IRISH FAIRY FORTS

First published 2025 by The O'Brien Press Ltd.,
12 Terenure Road East, Rathgar, Dublin 6, D06 HD27, Ireland.
Tel: +353 1 4923333; E-mail: books@obrien.ie. Website: obrien.ie
The O'Brien Press is a member of Publishing Ireland.
Reprinted 2025, 2026.

ISBN: 978-1-78849-501-1

9 8 7 6 5 4 3
29 28 27 26

Printed and bound by Drukarnia Skleniarz, Poland.
The paper in this book is produced using pulp from managed forests.

To the best of our knowledge, this book complies in full with the requirements
of the General Product Safety Regulation (GPSR). For further information
and help with any safety queries, please contact us at productsafety@obrien.ie.

IRISH FAIRY FORTS

PORTALS TO THE PAST

JO KERRIGAN AND RICHARD MILLS

THE O'BRIEN PRESS
DUBLIN

JO KERRIGAN was born and bred in Cork, where she took her first two degrees at UCC before moving to the UK to continue her academic work. After a distinguished career there, including winning the Oxbow Prize for medieval history at Oxford, she returned to her roots to apply her research skills to Ireland's undiscovered past. A specialist in ancient crafts and folklore, she now devotes herself to exploring how everyday life was lived long ago.

RICHARD MILLS was born in Provence, and moved to Ireland at the age of sixteen. His long and successful career as a press photographer was combined with a passion for wildlife, and his pictures have garnered numerous national and international awards. He was the subject of a TV programme by the wildlife film-maker Éamon de Buitléar, and he has contributed images to hundreds of publications across the world, as well as his own popular book, *Ireland's Bird Life: A World of Beauty*.

Jo and Richard live in West Cork, surrounded by books and cameras, cats and dogs. Previous books for O'Brien Press include *West Cork: A Place Apart*, *Old Ways, Old Secrets*; *Follow the Old Road*; *Brehon Laws*; *Stories From the Sea*; and *All The Way By The Grand Canal*.

Dedication

To na Daoine Mhaithe, the Good People, our ancient gods and spirits, who continue to watch over and care for this island of Ireland, this book is most respectfully dedicated.

CONTENTS

Acknowledgements and Note on Sources

Tribute must be paid to the incredible foresight of the Irish government of the 1930s. They set up the Folklore Commission, established to record our legends, beliefs, folklore and local customs. Schoolchildren were tasked with obtaining the knowledge of their older relatives and friends and writing it down. It was perhaps the most creative and visionary of that very new government's projects and resulted in a collection of immense value to researchers and historians everywhere.

This bank of priceless information, known as the Schools Collection, is now under the aegis of duchas.ie and has profited immeasurably from the hard work (still continuing) of volunteers who transcribe all these fascinating individual stories and transfer them online, making them available worldwide. Praise and thanks are due to every one of those volunteers.

Material from the Schools Collection has been much utilised within this book, but it was matched by the wonderful willingness of local people all over the country to share their own beliefs and knowledge of folklore. Wherever we went, we found everyone keenly interested in the research we were carrying out, and only too pleased to share what they knew. Thank you all.

That great historian and folklorist, Shane Lehane, was very willing to share his time in discussing the different facets of the old beliefs; and the work of Eddie Lenihan, folklorist and protector of the old ways par excellence, was an inspiration.

It should be noted that many of the sites mentioned within this book are on private land, and in cases where the exact location is not given, it is because the landowner expressly asked us not to. Always check and ask permission before visiting any ancient site.

Finally, it may well be pushing our luck even to mention this, but, quite apart from the welcome we received everywhere in the human sphere, a strange number of unusual small problems and accidents occurred throughout our wide-ranging fieldwork, which made us wonder if somebody – or something – was expressing annoyance at our interference with things that are best left alone. If so, and the Good People were responsible, please accept our sincere and respectful apologies. We have dedicated this book appropriately, as a form of compensation.

A perfectly circular ringfort, made by drawing
a circle around a central stick.

CHAPTER I

WHAT ARE FAIRY FORTS?

You will glimpse them, perhaps quite by chance, as you drive along country roads. Unusual grassy circles; strange, tree-covered mounds in the centre of otherwise smoothly tilled fields; the road making a sudden and unexpected diversion around an obstacle that certainly isn't a rock before returning to its straight route. Once you have got your eye in, so to speak, you will identify dozens of them. Very frequently (given our gentle climate and the enthusiastic willingness of bramble and bush to swallow up anything that stands still for more than a minute), they are too overgrown for you to be certain of what you are seeing. OS maps, unfortunately, rarely show fairy forts, although megaliths and other ancient archaeological features are usually well marked.

It is a good idea to consult Google Earth (an extremely recent invention when set against the timescale involved in these features). On Google Earth, these enigmatic earthworks stand out vividly – very clear circular formations in our otherwise squared and fenced environment. They are also often still clearly visible amid the gorse and bushes of wilder upland slopes.

Enormous numbers of fairy forts survive across Ireland. Somewhere between 45,000 and 60,000 is a very rough estimate, but in all probability there are many more, given the speed with which our lush vegetation covers up everything. However, advances in modern technology allow us to scan the landscape (and below it) more and more, and with considerably more accuracy than was ever possible heretofore, so the figure is likely to increase exponentially as ever more work is done.

So many ringforts within signalling distance of each other.

Never step inside a fairy ring. You may not be able to leave again.

Just a side note: don't confuse fairy forts with fairy rings, which are circles of mushrooms or fungi that spring up overnight, seemingly by magic, and last a very short time. They are said to mark places where the fairies have been dancing the night before. Temporary and delightful, they should be noted and enjoyed. However, don't venture into one, as that carries risks.

'I remember going out one morning and finding three large perfect circles of mushrooms in a field near us at home,' recalls Gobnait, who grew up in north Offaly. 'They were only in that one field, nowhere else. I went home and told my father, and he immediately said, "You didn't step inside one, did you?" I said no, and he said, relieved, "Oh, that's good. You might find you were in another place or another time altogether, and never be able to leave it again."' It's a widespread belief.

A point to note here, though, and one to which this book will return again, is that both fairy forts and fairy rings are circles, never square. The circle is one of the oldest and most powerful symbols in the world, and was especially important to those who dwelt in ancient Ireland. The evidence of its influence can be seen in many surviving features from those times, including not only the aforementioned forts and rings, but also stone citadels, round towers, beehive huts, and of course the magnificent archaeological structures in which this country is so rich, like those at Brú na Bóinne. Even old Irish graveyards were always built in the round, never square or oblong like those of later settlers.

An old Irish graveyard, circular instead of square or oblong.

The circle has of course been central to many religions and beliefs around the world, evolving naturally from observance of the turning of the year, the movement of crops through growth to harvest and disappearance into the earth, only to emerge again anew. Communities living close to nature, as most did in ancient times, would have observed the sun in its progress across the sky every day, going out of sight at night only to return the following morning; the moon waxing and waning over the month, and its effect on the tides; the constantly repeated slow dance of the cyclical round. To build shelters, homes and ritual sites in the same circular pattern was as natural as life itself.

The circle is a powerful form, as practitioners of wicca and other pagan religions know well. Casting a circle, whether for protection against evil influences or to create a charm, is the first thing you do when channelling what power you may need to achieve some important end. Drawing it with salt or white pebbles, lighting differently coloured candles at each point of the compass, or simply making a mental circle to aid concentration, are all familiar to those who work in the old ways. The vital thing is that the circle is unbroken, with no gap left to break the energy or allow malevolent energies to enter.

In ancient Ireland, as in many other venerable cultures, the circle was seen as reflecting the unending Wheel of Life, and was thus reflected and indeed respected in all early building.

As indicated above, even huge and impressive old stone forts or citadels (usually identified as dúns, caiseals, or cathairs), built and occupied over generations by powerful chieftains and kings or used as assembly and inauguration sites, were always circular. In a royal fort, the ruler was expected to live in some state, to welcome visitors, entertain them and offer good accommodation. For that you needed a large establishment with not only state rooms and a banqueting hall, but also homes for all the support systems – bakers, scribes, metalworkers and a myriad of other servants, as well as herders and their flocks. In addition, the regents of Ireland's provinces went on frequent journeys around their kingdoms, bringing with them their entourage, including their chief bard and chief Brehon or expert in the law. The people of one particular area would gather together at one of these well-known sites on the chosen day or number of days, to make known their disputes or complaints and have judgement given on the advice of the learned Brehon. All of this took place within the curving power of an unbroken circle, which strengthened and enforced the ceremony.

Even crannógs, those wonderfully photogenic little artificial islands built on wooden piles in lakes as sheltered homesteads of farmers, were carefully built in the round. Usually reached by boat or occasionally by a drawbridge that could be raised in times of danger, they were a practical design, and are still beautiful to see in our inland waters, now often covered with trees and appearing almost to float on the calm surface. Our little beehive huts, some of the oldest of which are still to be seen standing in remote places like Slea Head in Kerry, are so skilfully built in the round that you wonder how on earth they managed with only rounded stones to hand. Yet they were still being built in exactly the same way on islands like the Blaskets well into the nineteenth century.

A picturesque crannóg on a lake.

The greater caiseals are for the most part preserved, well maintained, open and accessible as tourist attractions. The looming grandeur of Staigue Fort in its deserted Kerry valley, for example; the spectacularly sited Dún Aengus on Inishmore in the Aran Islands; the magnificent Grianán of Aileach, arrogantly bestriding a Donegal hillside; Navan Fort or Emain Macha towering above Armagh. They have been researched and documented, and we do at least have some idea of their history, of who lived there and what battles might have taken place around them. The royal fort at Rathangan in Co. Kildare was even the subject of one of our oldest Irish poems.

Staigue Fort in Kerry, built in the Iron Age as a defensive stronghold for a local king.

The fort over against the oak-wood,
Once it was Bruidge's, it was Cathal's,
It was Aed's, it was Ailill's,
It was Conaing's, it was Cuilíne's,
And it was Maeldúin's.
The fort remains after each in its turn
And the kings asleep in the ground
(Kuno Meyer translation, 1913)

In many cases, later structures, and eventually Norman castles, were built on the sites of such original stone forts. These locations were chosen for the very same reasons as the originals – a good strategic point on a height, positioned to keep an eye on the countryside all round and give early warning of approaching visitors or enemies. It is not unusual to find a modern farmhouse on a high mound where centuries of earlier buildings have stood, each in turn decaying and giving way to the newer structure.

However, crannógs and beehive huts, and the larger caiseals and dúns, have not, for some reason, gathered to themselves the countless legends, superstitions and beliefs that fairy forts have. Why this is, we simply don't know. But it's a fact. Admired, yes; snapped a thousand times, certainly. But venerated and feared? No.

Real fairy forts or fairy mounds are far smaller than any cathair though. They do not in any way resemble kingly residences like Dún Aengus or Staigue, except in that vital circular shaping. So what exactly are they?

These little features are to be found everywhere in the Irish countryside. They occasionally have a stone encircling wall, but more commonly merely an earthen ditch, often overgrown and covered with hawthorn, gorse and enthusiastic brambles. A few will have two or even three protective ditches and banks surrounding the central circle, but often these have been eroded by time or filled in by usage of the surrounding fields. The enclosed space may be no wider than fifteen metres or, rarely, may be as extensive as forty metres. (Incidentally, in the ancient Brehon laws, the dimensions dictated for the residence of a tribal king, which would certainly have been a caiseal or dún, was c.140 feet, or 42.56 metres.)

So numerous are they, and so long have they been part of the landscape, that they are virtually taken for granted by local residents (with certain careful provisos, as we will see). Known in Irish as ráths or lios, the briefest glance through a topographical directory or map will show that such features, both the large imposing ones and the smaller ones, though they are not individually identified as a rule, have given their names to innumerable townlands, villages and locations. They have thus remained very much a part of our modern landscape.

Just some examples: Lissarda (the high fort), Lisdoonvarna (the lios at the fort of the gap, a nice example of lios and dún combined in the same place name), Lisduff, Lismore, Liosnapuca. Lisnakea in Co. Fermanagh means 'the fort of the sceach or whitethorn tree'. It took its name from the celebrated Sceach-ghabhra [Skagowra], under which the Maguire leaders were traditionally inaugurated. Rathmore (the large fort), between Millstreet and Killarney. The town and railway station hug the main road, but south of the conurbation in a quiet field

This way to the lios at the fort of the gap.

lies the original Ráth Mór that gave the place its name. Every time the train passes Charleville in Co. Cork, the conductor announces in Irish 'An Ráth', which is its proper name, commemorating the ancient ringfort. Rathdangan, Rathpeacon, Ratheenduff (the little black fort), Raheenroe or Raithin-ruadh (the little red fort). And there are hundreds more to be discovered in every county.

Dúns and caiseals are equally numerous, although you might not realise at first what a signpost is telling you. Dunmore, Dun Laoghaire (the fort of Laoghaire), Dunmanway, Dunbeacon, Dunboyne, Dunbrody – the list is endless. Even

Ráth Mór ringfort near Rathmore.

the great rock of Cashel itself preserves forever in its Irish name, An Caiseal, the memory of its mighty past as the palace of the King of Munster (it passed into the hands of the Christian clergy in later times). All reflect old memories and strong tradition surrounding places of powerful magic.

Westmeath: In Adamstown at the back of Martin Neill's house there is a fort circled with clay and stones. In Mr Casey's field there is a fort called Ráth Drishóg. It is a big hill circled with rocks. The townland still bears the name Ráth Drishóg. In Jack Pigot's field, Killeen, there is a high fort surrounded with banks. In the middle of it the fairies thatched their little houses with feathers.

So what do academic experts say about these so-called fairy forts? The formal archaeological approach classifies them (quite correctly) as old enclosures, constructed of either turf or stone, depending on what the local environment most easily offered, and used to shelter humans and their animals both from the weather and against threats from raiders or wild beasts such as wolves, which were plentiful here in earlier times. These enclosures were most likely made in their traditionally circular shape by the simple act of attaching a súgán rope (made by twisting straw) to a central stick and drawing a large circle.

As we have already seen, circles were always the instinctive shape in ancient Ireland. The harder square and oblong designs came in with later invaders, who did not have the same respect for the natural return of things to their beginning before starting off again. Perhaps it was the increasing availability of bricks rather than the materials that were naturally to hand in the landscape that effected this change. But then we remember Egypt's pyramids and other ancient buildings across the world, all angles and edges, and must consider that it was a different way of thinking, a sternly practical approach rather than the instinctive, emotive approach of a land and its people working in harmony with each other. A circular enclosure was easy to create with that stick and rope, but wouldn't a square or oblong shape be as easy to mark out?

The fact remains that all ancient Irish structures were carefully built in the round, honouring a belief and a tradition as old as time itself. An early Irish burial ground is instantly recognisable by its ring shape, while the later, Christian ones are square or oblong, as are their buildings.

It is hard to tell what the interiors of these circular enclosures might have looked like, given the centuries of change in between. Certainly any enclosure used for protection would have needed lookout points or at least a high centre, as well as flat spaces for huts. Whatever their size or the materials used, they would have taken a lot of hard labour and considerable time to erect. What we see today as a hollowed space within an earthwork probably contained a central mound ten thousand years ago. Indeed, that they have lasted so long, albeit much reduced and eroded by the passage of many centuries, is tribute to their original builders.

The huts or houses within a ráth or lios would have been built simply of posts with interlaced rods and coverings of reeds or straw, while in a grander dún or caiseal stone would have been used. There would also have been shelters within the central space for livestock. (It would have been asking for trouble to let your precious sheep or cattle roam free across the hillsides at night, what with roaming bands of wolves and opportunistic raiders from nearby settlements on the lookout for easy prey.)

Unsurprisingly, very little evidence remains of these original layouts, but archaeological excavation has yielded enough information to enable several excellent reconstructions to be built, for example at Lough Gur in Limerick and the Irish National Heritage Park in Wexford. Such developments can really bring you back into the past and give you some idea of

A reconstruction of ancient dwellings at Lough Gur.

what life was like so long ago. Today, when so many children grow up in urban environments, with no idea that anything could exist that didn't come from a shop or supermarket, these archaeological reconstructions are very valuable, especially on open days when ancient crafts and skills may be demonstrated.

It can be frankly confusing at first to sort through the enormous range of differentiations in archaeology-speak – some separate hill and promontory forts from inland ringforts, henges from dúns and caiseals, barrows from ditch pit circles; while others insist on separating stone-built from earthen enclosures. Even the experts can't agree on a fixed scheme of assigning a landscape feature firmly to one or other of these categories, and it is unlikely they will do so while so many remain hidden, unexcavated or much altered from their

You catch sight of them everywhere. An old ringfort in a field.

original forms. It isn't worth agonising over. In this book, as already indicated, we are talking about the little ones, built either of earth or stone, almost disappeared into the landscape today but still retaining a powerful presence.

Even the common usage of the descriptive term 'fort' is questionable. A fort is usually taken to mean a strong, fortified, defensive structure, and most fairy forts were anything but that. It is strange to place a tiny, grassy circle in a field in the same category as the splendour of An Grianán or Staigue, but 'fort' is the accepted term, so we might as well go along with it. (No, you can't call it a fairy ring – that term belongs strictly to the mushroom circles that spring up overnight and disappear just as quickly.) Throughout this book we will refer to a fort, ráth, lios, dún or caiseal as seems appropriate, or where others have used those terms.

Arguments also continue in archaeological circles as to how far back these structures date, but while some are content to say 'medieval or thereabouts', the current trend is to move at least some of them well back into prehistory. It is, in fact, pretty difficult to date something made of timeless earth and stones. Quite often an arbitrary century is allocated based on what has been found in an excavation. If artefacts are recovered, and these can be dated fairly accurately, then the structure itself is usually given the same date, although that is hardly satisfactory, given that such places might well have been occupied for many generations. Such a questionable solution can be likened to discovering the most up-to-date smartphone in a crumbling old house, and immediately deciding that the house was built only yesterday! It's never that simple. Let's just say that some of our still-extant fairy forts were certainly here well before Christianity ever came tramping determinedly over the horizon.

We know this because they are mentioned in the oldest writings, which themselves came into being when the zealous, newly arrived monks started to record in script the oral history of this land, carried through countless previous generations by the druids and bards, and passed down from the old to the young. Written records date from the fifth century AD onwards, but the knowledge and information they contain go back into the mists of time.

The Dindsenchas or Lore of Places is one such record, in which the wise ones shared their information with the scribes so long ago. It has many references to these magical sites, showing not only that they were a familiar sight to the druids, but that they were, even then (for at least several centuries before the arrival of the monks), regarded as ancient. For example:

Sinand … Mongan's daughter from the fairy dwellings …
… a prince's son, the fairest that dwelt in a fairy mound in Erin …
… He was the craftsman of Badbh's fairy mound …

References like this demonstrate just how far back the tradition goes of regarding these places as the dwelling places of the Good People. It isn't a recent belief, the product of a modern desire for romance or mystery, but a very old conviction indeed, which has never died out.

'Gentle' is a term you often find in the stories and legends about these magical structures. Lena Connolly of Mullinasole in Donegal used that word quite naturally when sharing her knowledge of local places back in the 1930s:

The fairies must have liked Mullinasole very much because there are quite a number of gentle spots within reach of our home. On the hill behind James Likely's house there are two gentle spots and on Hugh Martin's hill which lies right above James Likely's hill there are four fairy mounds. There is a big hole under the ground stretching from one of the mounds in James Likely's field to the big mound in Hugh Martin's field. It is three and a half feet deep and it is one quarter of a mile long.

Souterrains or underground tunnels are indeed common to many of these forts. Used for storage, for shelter, perhaps even for escape, there are many records of tunnels leading for long distances underneath, even linking two similar rings. It is not unusual to find such souterrains in larger forts, where raids and battles might well be expected, which extend a long way to a safe exit. Such were the times in which the occupants lived.

There is an old fort in Droumalonhart in the west of Glencar [Co. Kerry]. There is a big hole down in the ground and stepping stones going down. Under the ground are two rooms. These are made of gravel.
    A fort is a round raised up piece of earth with a ring of trees around it. The fairies were supposed to live in them long ago.

Some of these forts have under ground tunnels or passages lead-ing from one to another.

The tunnels are six or seven mile long. These passages or tunnels are called coves and are supposed to have been used by the fairies long ago. It is wrong to clear these forts or to touch them in any way. A fort is made about one hundred and thirty yards in circumference. It is a lonely place and people do not like to go near it at night.

The most of them are a round shape. There is a bank of earth around some of them and stones around more of them. There are trees around a few of them.

Outside one of them is a hole, going down into the ground with steps down into it. The people say that that is the entrance into it. Nobody ever went down that hole.

It is circular in shape surrounded by a mound of earth, outside which there is a circle of trees. In the centre of it is an entrance hole. Anyone that went in there never came out again …

Today, unsurprisingly, most of these souterrains still existing are completely blocked up, since the risk they pose to both human and animal life cannot be denied. Children disappearing without trace; animals falling in and breaking a leg; daring explorers getting lost – it is understandable, although a pity that we can no longer see many of them. Some that were strongly built with stone walls and roofs are still to be found in parts of the country, but always with protective gates and warnings. We live in different times.

In archaeological thinking, this is generally where these enigmatic circles have been left. Earthen or stone enclosures, used sometimes for habitation, more often for gathering cattle. Sometimes deep holes or tunnels found in them. No particular dates; no major discoveries. No links to heroic figures of old, no stirring tales of battle or romance. Taken for granted. Just old enclosures. Nothing to see here, move on.

Not good enough. Emphatically not good enough. There is no such thing as 'just' in history or its place in the landscape. No object or unusual feature should be left at what is only a starting point. Always lift it up metaphorically, peer under it, check around it, ask the questions begging to be asked by virtue of its very existence. Why might it have been built? Approximately when? By whom? These are all reasonable questions, and most of us will have voiced or at least thought those queries at one time or another. However, one other huge question above all emerges from the fact that these are the most numerous archaeological features still found in modern, developed Ireland.

So, what is the huge question?

HOW COME THEY ARE STILL HERE IN SUCH ENORMOUS NUMBERS?

The Ireland of today, like most other countries, is constantly moving forward, planning, clearing, building, commercialising. More housing is demanded year by year, more roads, more services. Villages expand into towns, then into large residential conglomerations. The outcry for more space, more land on which to build homes, to develop lucrative industries, to extend the farms that supply the essential foodstuffs for a growing population as well as for export, is never-ending. It is ongoing right now, even as you read this.

Yet still these enigmatic little green mounds and circles remain, untouched, often in the very centre of a rigorously farmed landscape, surrounded by crops and cattle. Old laneways and minor roads curve carefully around them instead of taking the easy route straight through. Even modern motorways are diverted to avoid touching them. Plans for new factories are amended, layouts shifted, to take account of these far-longer-established features in the countryside.

What is the power that fairy forts hold even in today's world of cynical planners, ambitious companies, demanding

The motorway and access roads had to respect this fairy fort near Nenagh.

populations? Because hold it they certainly do. Look at those figures again: There are up to 60,000 fairy forts still here in the landscape, in an otherwise rapidly changing Ireland. Forests may fall, fields may disappear under housing estates, far-reaching views may become obscured by development, once-peaceful countryside may echo to the roar of traffic, but the fairy forts remain.

And the reason they remain is more powerful than any government plan or any ambitious development project. It has its endless, intertwining, interlacing roots buried deep in the very nature and character of Ireland. What is the real truth behind the amazing survival of our fairy forts?

Fairy fort meets adjoining hedgerows but doesn't yield.

CHAPTER II

THE POWER OF BELIEF

For centuries, the ancient fairy forts of Ireland have been believed to be the homes of na Daoine Mhaithe, the Good People, also known respectfully as Themselves, the Gentry or even, affectionately, the Other Crowd.

Why is this? Or, more accurately, why has it always been so, since the belief has stood firm for millennia? Well, according to folklore (and remember, folklore means the lore of the people, the history that has been passed down through memory from one generation to another, where no written record exists), it has to do with the Tuatha dé Danann, who held Ireland long long ago, and the Celts or Milesians, who later came up from Spain with the firm intention of seizing the fertile island for themselves. It is said that the warlike, wandering Celts had long known of this green land in the far northwest. They were determined to reach it if they could, travelling halfway across the world in search of their goal. The last leap was from northern Spain, and then they were here, ready to do battle and take over.

The Tuatha dé Danann (the People of Danu, the mother goddess) are said to have been a tall, fair and courtly race, fond of music, feasting and the arts, and skilled in magic. They had lived here for a long time, devoted to the care of Ireland's landscape and its fertility. When the Celts arrived, the Tuatha dé Danann fought bravely for the place they loved, but after some time, their leaders realised that endless battles did no good for anyone, least of all for the land they protected. They therefore sought to reach an agreement with the invaders, suggesting that they each take half of the island, and thereby peacefully co-exist. In this way, Ireland itself would suffer no more harm.

Unfortunately, the Celts had cunning leaders, well versed in the strategies and counter-movements of war, and they managed to manoeuvre the agreement so that the half to be taken by the Tuatha dé Danann would actually lie below ground and below water. Realising they had been tricked, the former lords of the country, instead of fuming and heading straight back into battle, acted in accordance with their noble character. They decided that rather than lay waste to everything they cared for, they would accept the unfair ruling.

Using their magical arts, they thus withdrew from the upper world of Ireland into the hills and under the rivers, lakes and surrounding sea. There, in the Otherworld, they continue to live as before, a life of music, dancing and feasting. They occasionally emerge to visit each other in different parts of the country, or to see what the human population is up to, always maintaining their passionate love of Ireland and their care for its good health. They became, in fact, our spirit ancestors, the gods and goddesses of nature itself.

The fairy mounds, especially those with tunnels or souterrains lying underneath, are seen as entrances to this Otherworld, as are caves, hills, wells, springs, rivers and lakes – anywhere that can be seen to shield the world we know from the one we do not. They can be perceived as the gateways if you like, but it is most inadvisable to try passing through such a gateway without an official invitation.

This farmhouse track has carefully skirted its resident fairy fort.

This is such a strongly held belief that from one end of the country to the other, people will go well out of their way to avoid interfering with or damaging these special places in any way. More, they will warn others to desist from such attempts, should they hear of any such plans, believing it their duty so to do. Interference could include removing stones from a fort for building purposes; digging for treasure (the belief that there are vast fortunes of gold and jewels hidden under such places is well-nigh universal); grazing cattle or sheep in the enclosure; or cutting for fuel the bushes and trees that have self-rooted in and around the fort. Indeed, the hawthorn tree (which is a powerful fairy tree, and should never be moved from wherever it chooses to place itself) is also known as a scióg, or fairy bush.

Incidentally, the term 'fairies' is mostly used only in English cultural traditions, most of which were created during an upsurge of passionate interest in the subject in the early twentieth century. This was sparked by the appearance of a series of photographs that became known as the Cottingley Fairies, purporting to show the elusive little creatures perched on trees and playing with two little girls. Even such noted writers as Sir Arthur Conan Doyle believed in them, and JM Barrie's creation of Tinkerbell in his play *Peter Pan* established once and for all the English perception of these beings. The Flower Fairies paintings by Cicely Mary Barker, first published in 1923, did much to consolidate this perception. The revelation, as late as the 1980s, that the Cottingley Fairies were a hoax, cleverly created from scrapbooks by the two little girls as a joke, did nothing to remove that firm equation of 'fairy' with tiny flying charmers.

The Irish would rarely speak of the Otherworld inhabitants in such terms, using instead respectful titles such as the Good People or the Gentry. (The one exception might be in the expression 'away with the fairies', a common phrase in use even today, as in, 'Ah, sure, he's away with the fairies!' This means that someone is so detached from reality, whether temporarily or as a general habit, that he or she must have been touched by Themselves.)

The Irish Good People then, it should be made clear from the outset, are very far from the cute little flower fairies of Victorian illustrations. They are not little pantomime heroines, nor helpful brownies, and neither are they growling goblins, terrifying trolls or even the pestiferous piskies of Cornwall, who exist just to cause trouble. They are a powerful people, our ancient earth spirits, gods and goddesses who care for the land, not little creatures who pop up to lend a hand or make mischief. Indeed, they keep themselves very much to themselves, only interacting with the human world when it suits them – to inveigle away a good-looking young man, for instance; to enter on a love tryst with a beautiful girl; or even to snatch a baby from its cradle to add to their own domain.

The Irish know these qualities of their Otherworld neighbours instinctively and are always careful to show proper respect. As explained above, they are in fact the Tuatha dé Danann, godlike people who were driven into their underground domain by the bellicose Celts. There they remain to this day. We will meet them more fully in Chapter V.

The strong belief, everywhere prevalent even in today's ultra-modern Ireland, is that fairy forts should always be left alone. On no account are they to be interfered with or damaged in any way. On all sides, you will hear warnings and expressions of fear as to what might happen if you were unwise enough to cross swords with Themselves. The Schools Collection, that superb gathering of lore and legends from the 1930s, is crammed with these warnings:

It is believed that there were some good kind people in the forts and that they used to visit the people living near them. If they were treated kindly and got anything they asked, they were harmless. On the other hand they were supposed to seek terrible vengeance on anyone who did them any injury.

The owners of the land in which they are situated never interfere with them or plant crops in them. The old people say that it is not lucky to touch them or cut the trees around them as they are supposed to be haunted.

The old people used to say that nobody should go near a fort alone.

The owners of the land where the forts are never interfere with them when ploughing or planting crops nor will any one cut down or interfere with the trees surrounding it.

Any person who ever as much as cut a bush or rod from this fort never was much the better. They either lost cattle or something happened to themselves …

They are held in awe by the folks around so much so that they would never interfere with them for fear of misfortune befalling themselves or their cattle.

None of the inhabitants of these districts ever interfere with these forts, as it is considered unlucky to do so.

It is said that fairies live in them and that they are to be seen at twelve o'clock at night. It is also said that they fix boots in the forts. When farmers are ploughing or tilling a field in which there is a fort they will not interfere with it or cut down a bush or tree belonging to it as they consider it unlucky.

The old people, because they believed the fairies lived in the Lioses, were very careful about them and never cut trees or bushes on them. They would not eat a rabbit caught in or near a Lios. When a farmer meant to plough a Lios he never did so without first turning a sod and left it until the day after. If the sod was turned back in the morning he left the Lios unploughed.

Specific prohibitions vary a little from one area to another. Some believe you should never enter a fairy fort; others say it is all right to cut hay within their circle, or even graze small flocks there, as long as you do no damage to trees or shrubs.

Elderly Billy, leaning on the pub counter in a country village, twinkles cheerfully. 'Ah I'd never go to damage a fairy fort. We were always taught never to do that.' He considers for a moment. 'But wait now while I remember. There was that winter not long ago when we had the big storm. Well a tree fell from the ráth and lay right across the field. We talked about it, and then my brother said it should be all right to cut it up, now that it was fallen and out of the place itself. He did that, and stacked the wood away, and it's burning fine in his stove now. So far we haven't had any repercussions, but that's because it fell away from the place and was separated from it, d'you see?'

It is also believed that you should leave a share of what you harvest or gather for Themselves, whether it's putting a tempting little saucer of food outside the kitchen door at night or turning an understanding eye to a cow that has strayed into a fairy fort and returned somehow milked dry. At great festivals like Samhain, food is traditionally laid out after the family has gone to bed, in case the Otherworld spirits feel hungry, or our own ancestors return to see we are running the place as it should be.

There is a fort over Patrick Mc Entee's house. One day, when he was very young, his mother was taking the butter off the churn. Patrick had a porringer and he was throwing out buttermilk round the door. The mother lifted her hand and went down and gave him a slap. When she was returning, she heard a voice saying, 'Why do you beat the child for giving me a drink?' She looked round and saw a little red woman who disappeared.

Everywhere you go, and with everyone you ask, it's the same story. They may deny all knowledge of fairy forts, but that strictest of old beliefs remains – always show respect, never insult, never invade or damage.

Never fall into the error of thinking that these are simply 'old ways, old beliefs' and dismissing them as coming from a foolish age of myth and superstition. All too many have a mistaken confidence these days that modern science has solved everything, and that older traditions have no place in our world. Not so. The conviction that you should never damage

This ringfort among heavy industrial development remains untouched.

or interfere with a fairy fort is as strong now as ever it was, and not just among country folk, but among all walks of life and in every corner of the land.

'Of course I wouldn't touch one,' says John, a senior consultant at a huge urban hospital. 'I would stand back, admire, honour it if you like, but I would never damage it. It's just something you don't do.' Pressed for a reason, he says simply that he has always known this. 'I suppose my parents must have passed that belief down to me.'

Paddy, an eminent dentist in a city practice, concurs. 'I remember being taken for walks around a local one when we were young, but my father always warned us not to interfere with them or cut anything. They were ancient monuments, he said, and deserving of our respect.'

'They're not for us to interfere with,' insists Peadar Ó Riada, a renowned composer and musician. 'They come from a different era, and just because we can't understand them, that doesn't give us the right to do what we like with them.'

And so on, right to the country folk who live cheek by jowl with these mysterious relics of the past. 'Damage a fairy fort? Indeed no, and I wouldn't,' says Ger, a postman. 'That would be very bad luck indeed – and bad manners too!'

'We were always taught never to go inside the neighbouring fairy fort on the farm next to where we grew up,' says Bríd. 'The people on whose land it was warned us that it would bring bad fortune if we invaded the territory of Themselves, and we followed their advice. You wouldn't even pick blackberries inside there!' And that, from a country girl accustomed to harvesting the hedgerows for their bounty, is saying something.

'You'd never go to damage a fairy fort, or take stones from it or anything,' says Breda who runs a busy family hotel and restaurant. 'Of course you wouldn't. That would be inviting bad luck, so it would.'

John, a quiet-spoken man managing a garden centre, at first says, when asked, that he knows nothing about fairy forts. Then he pauses. 'There is one thing I do know, though, and that is I'd never interfere with one. That would be inviting trouble.'

That is the typical reply on all sides today. Some people will disclaim all knowledge and deny they know any stories about fairy forts, but ask them if they would damage it, remove anything, level it if it were in their way, and the answer never changes. No, definitely not. It would be bad luck. Asked then how they know this, and usually they will stop, think for a moment and then say, 'But that's the way of it – it always has been.' Most recall being warned by their parents never to do anything to offend Themselves or the entrances to the Otherworld – the local ráths or lios.

That belief in the power and strength of the fairy fort goes a long, long way back, into the mists of prehistory. Academics, as we mentioned in Chapter I, have dated these forts variously from medieval times to as late as the eighteenth century, but many have existed far longer. For proof, see the Dindsenchas, already mentioned briefly in Chapter I.

Incorporating as it does some of our oldest pagan mythology, the Dindsenchas or Lore of Places has proved of immense value in establishing what was already known – had been known for thousands of years, having been handed down from generation to generation by word of mouth – before the Roman religion brought the custom of recording with ink on vellum to our shores. And the fairy forts or mounds are actually mentioned in many of these legends. This shows not only how far back the belief in them goes, but also, extremely importantly, that they were regarded as already ancient even when those records were composed by the bards and druids, let alone the far later documenting by the Christian Church around the sixth century AD. It can cause a shiver to read:

She was not mastered by a spell, but by the doleful music from the fairy mounds …

… and to realise that this is the voice of a druid or bard speaking across the ages from many centuries before the birth of Christ, and that he or she (yes, women were both druids and bards in those enlightened days) knew them to have existed from long before their own time.

The lios, the ráth, the fairy fort, then, was here in our land in great numbers long before the creation of fields and hedges. And each has stayed exactly where it was originally built,

Carefully maintained fields surround it, but this ringfort is not interfered with.

taking no heed of later development around it. But that the people who developed the land took heed of it is obvious. All over the country, you will see examples of careful acknowledgement of the ancient site. Banks, ditches and hedgerows come right up to the far older circle and stop there; they do not break the ring. It is common to see three or four – even five – fields converge at such a location, with the lios or ráth calmly holding its original place and identity entirely unchanged in the centre.

Even more common is the sight of a circular mound looking oddly out of place right in the middle of a huge and otherwise smoothly tilled field. Crops are a vital source of income for the farmer, but he would not think of cutting into or damaging that reminder of other times, that repository of ancient ways. There it stays, and his plough or reaper makes careful circles around it, year after year. Yes, it would offer quite a bit of valuable extra land for crops, and with today's equipment, digging it up, removing it completely wouldn't be a very big physical problem. However, he knows instinctively that he would be inviting trouble in other ways. And so he leaves it in peace.

In Streedagh, Co. Sligo, the story is still remembered of when the lands of a deceased farmer were divided amongst local people in the early 1930s. 'Between every two men's shares the Land Commission erected a fence of earth,' said Kathleen McGowan. 'One of these fences was to pass across the fort, but the people to whom the land was given would not interfere with the fort, so the fence was built around it.' That ancient earthwork still stands, surrounded by five fields. It's the same with the great old ráth at Rathmore in Co. Kerry, mentioned in Chapter I. The fort stands proud, the fields bow in submission and keep their place outside its boundaries.

Another very visible sign of the care with which these old structures have always been treated is the discovery of a farm track, a lane, even a major road making a deliberate circuit around it rather than cutting through. One might well appreciate that a wise countryman, knowledgeable in the old ways, would choose to go around rather than through this ancient monument he has inherited from his forefathers, but seeing the National Roads Authority (NRA) doing the same is

Grange ringfort at the junction of five fields near Streedagh. Local farmers would not damage it.

more surprising. And yet it still happens. Local pressure in most cases will simply not allow such a transgression, and the people of the area under threat are not afraid to take on the big boys of progress.

In the twenty-first century, the pressure for ever more land to build houses, factories and industrial sites increases by the day, putting ever more pressure on our ancient ringforts. But there are always valiant voices to be heard. Believers continue to come forward, doing their utmost to prevent such vandalism – for vandalism it surely is – and warn of the consequences.

One very recent example: In 2015, a large American pharmaceutical company announced it was going to build a new factory in Waterford, right on the site of the renowned triple-walled Knocklong fairy fort, estimated to be thousands of years old. (It is thought that less than three percent of Ireland's fairy forts are trivallate and the importance of this one at Knocklong was beyond dispute.) Countless objections flooded in, among them the sharp warning of historian and folklore expert Eddie Lenihan, who said that ill luck would follow anyone involved in damaging the ancient lios. 'It's a question of when, and not if, the fairies will decide to take their revenge,' he said. Local construction workers listened to the advice that came in on all sides, and refused to remove the fort.

However, in this case the battle was ultimately lost: the determined company drafted in teams from elsewhere, and the site was cleared in 2017 to make way for the new industrial complex. Time will tell what the consequences of this might be … We will meet other examples of modern development meeting ancient belief in Chapter VII, Hidden in the Landscape.

Happily, we can enjoy one very endearing example of damage to a fairy fort being unavoidable, but where the authorities did all they could (and a little bit more) to compensate for the injury.

If you cross from Cork into Kerry on the N22 towards Killarney, you will see carved stone sculptures at intervals – most notably a rearing Celtic war horse, complete with horned helmet and broken dangling chains, showing that it has broken free from tyranny, at the very point where the dramatic mountainscape of the Kingdom opens out in front of you. These works of art were created utilising boulders quarried during the road works. They make this route a thing of beauty, as well as demonstrating that blasting and earthmoving in the name of progress can, if enough care and attention are given from the start, result in something permanently lovely as well as uplifting. They now stand amid carefully planned groves of native shrubs, trees and plants that play their part in returning the environment to something approaching its former balance.

Tadhg Ryan, a garden designer who was commissioned to oversee the landscaping, is also (perhaps unusually, perhaps not) a qualified psychotherapist. He sees these pieces of art as almost like acupuncture points. 'I've always had the instinctive urge to make damaged environments beautiful once more, as well as a lifelong interest in the Otherworld. I've a firm belief in nature, earth spirits, and the balance which must be maintained. We all know the legend of the Tuatha dé Danann, the ancient people of Ireland, who were faced with the implacable invaders, the Milesians/Celts. Rather than continue endless battles, which would have devastated the land they revered so much, they simply withdrew into that landscape – into the rocks and streams and earth – and became the Good People, dwelling in that Middle Kingdom and passing on to our forbears the instinctive respect and love for the land and sacred places.' And so he ensured that everything was planned to heal the savage scars left by such a development and encourage the landscape to regain its true balance.

But it is close to Killarney itself, in the townland of Clasheen, that you will find something so simple, so natural that you

Clasheen ringfort cut into on the N22 near Killarney.

might miss it if you weren't looking especially. A high wall runs along a straight stretch; and worked into the very stones you can see a series of circles – small, medium, large. Inside that wall is an old fairy fort, the rare kind with three surrounding ditches and banks, known as trivallate.

Risteard O'Lionaird, who was senior resident engineer on this section of the new road, explains the specially designed wall. 'To widen the road at this point, they found they would have to cut a slice from the side of that very ancient fairy fort or ráth. I really didn't want that to happen, and spoke several times with the designer, trying to get him to tweak the layout a bit to avoid the fort. He did try, but after looking at every possibility, said it just wasn't possible. So I accepted, reluctantly, that they would have to do that, but by way of healing and reparation, I got them to build the circles into the retaining wall, reflecting the triple defence walls of the fort. I measured those banks on the fort and the stone circles built into the walls are an exact reduced scale replica of the circles round the fort itself.'

He too says he has always cared for our heritage and was taught from childhood to respect and revere the old ráths and lios that dot the countryside. 'I felt that by creating this special wall I was giving something back to the fairies if you like, trying to show that we were apologising, doing what we could in reparation.' He reveals that even then there were problems. 'One of the young lads on the project just wouldn't have anything to do with damaging that fort. He said he couldn't and he wouldn't and that was that. So I had to give him by-leave. It caused a problem, I can tell you that, because he was the

The three ring designs on the wall at the fairy fort on the N22 near Killarney.

one driving the digger. But we managed in the end, without having to force somebody against his will to do what he believed was wrong.' Further evidence, if that were needed, of the continuation of belief, generation after generation.

Above the stone wall, the aged holly trees that circle the earthwork look calmly out at the passing traffic. Those holly trees, as well as other natives like rowan or mountain ash, hazel and oak, and vibrant shrubs like the lovely spindle, have also been planted along the route, taller trees in the richer land and tough shrubs in the thinner, stonier soil, to recreate the natural landscape as it would have been in times past. Touches like this make this new road unlike any other.

To see the damage that is necessarily caused by such development, and then take steps to soothe and heal the damaged landscape, is visionary indeed. And the route has proved safe and welcoming ever since. The Old Ones have been pleased to accept the compensation – or perhaps one should call it 'honour price' as they would have millennia ago – for the injury inflicted. All is peaceful once more. This is surely the way to go when major works are in the pipeline – showing care and thoughtfulness instead of blasting ahead and disregarding the damage being caused.

There is another side to fairy forts too, one you might not expect. Far from threatening, this role is far more protective and poignant. The Roman Catholic Church, in unbelievable cruelty, decreed around 400 AD that babies who died unbaptised could not be buried in consecrated ground. Many heartbroken parents interred the precious remains in a cillín, an unofficial burial ground, instead, placing a small stone on the tiny grave as a marker. There are, sadly, all too many of these cillíns dotted around the countryside, marked on OS maps. They serve as a reminder of just how brutal a powerful religion can be in its drive to keep its members in check.

It was Augustine who decreed that such unfortunate babies were doomed to the flames of Hell. (He most certainly has no claim to sainthood, given his misogynistic attacks on women and harshness towards those who did not conform to his implacable ideals.) This truly hideous diktat was softened in Church teaching of later centuries to a sort of non-existence known as Limbo, which in turn was abolished (not before time) in 1992. What a world that hath such religions in it!

Tiny gravestones in a ráth.

To those who believe in the ancient power of ancient places, it is genuinely heartening to see that some of these sad little cillíns were created in fairy forts. It clearly shows that sorrowing parents, denied the bleak comfort of a gravestone in officially consecrated ground, turned instead to the older, kinder gods, sure that they would open their arms to the little being and keep it safe. Their lost babies would be guarded by their spirit ancestors, who did not have the grasping authoritarianism of the much later religion.

Some people call them old ráths, and some lioses. They are not to be ploughed or touched only for the purpose of a small grave, for the children who were not baptized in the church.

In some fort-cillíns, the little graves have actually been grouped around a hawthorn, the acknowledged fairy tree, for extra protection. Visiting one of these sites, you cannot but feel the anguish of so many heartbroken parents, but you can also sense the strength and 'rightness' of beliefs that made them place their little lost ones here, where their sleep would not be disturbed.

One such cillín, near Ballaghadereen in Co. Roscommon, stands in the middle of a large, remote field, off a narrow grassy track. It is only visible when you actually walk through the gate and cross the rough ground. A tumbled stone wall surrounding a grassy circle comes into view, and then a gap in the stones enables you to climb into the centre. At the far side are a group of venerable thorn trees and a grassy mound. Walk over, prod that mound gently with a stick, and

Ballaghadereen fairy fort, where unbaptised children were buried beneath the hawthorn tree.

you will find many rounded stones, hidden from view, most no bigger than a baby's head. Stroke back the covering grass from one and lay your hand briefly in blessing on the stone thus revealed, before replacing its warm, grassy blanket and leaving it in peace. It is safe here.

'If you cut a bush in a fairy fort
you will have bad luck all year.'

CHAPTER III

DISTURB US AT YOUR PERIL!

On every side, from anyone you ask, and from all accounts recorded over the years, the same harsh, unnerving fact is taken as absolute. Bad things will happen if you interfere with a fairy fort.

It can be something as simple as the prick of a thorn that then turns very painful; a fire that refuses to light when laid with kindling taken from a lios. It can be more life-threatening, like a sudden illness or the breaking of a limb. It can be ruinous, like all your cattle dying or your home going up in a blaze. All these misfortunes and many more have passed into legend.

But are they just legends, told by the fire with fearful glances over the shoulder? Mere stories to inspire both fear and terrified delight among the listeners? Are they really believed today, or are they just remnants of a more innocent time, before the coming of electricity and modernisation banished the shadows lurking on the stairway for good and all?

Well, there will always be those who disbelieve, who are smugly ready with their own reasoned explanations for such happenings. Pure coincidence is the most popular one, closely followed by, 'Ah, sure the illness came on anyway, and they just decided to tie the two things up together.' 'Such things don't happen these days,' is another, offered by those with a touching confidence in the power of modern technology to solve all the mysteries that the natural world could ever offer. Cheerfully ignoring the fact that the weather and Nature will always continue to do whatever they want, these unbelievers turn back to the virtual images of television and social media and believe that they are looking at real existence.

It is rather hard to ignore, however, that unfortunate occurrences following closely on such invasions of a ráth, a lios, a fairy fort, seem to be way more numerous than normal coincidence or probability would allow. To put it plainly, there are just too many of them to be airily explained away. Certainly, those who have witnessed such events are in no doubt as to their Otherworldly cause. And you don't have to go back a century or more to find the anger of Themselves emphatically believed in. That belief is still very much with us today.

"Twas a farmer over the other side of the river,' begins a local man in a low voice, leaning on the gate and glancing around him in case he might be overheard. (You very often find this reluctance to share knowledge of such things openly, for fear of being laughed at.)

'He had this fairy fort on his land a while back, y'see, and he wanted to get rid of it, as he said it was spoiling his field

Fairy hill with guardian tree.

and he couldn't use the place to its best advantage. Well, his neighbours warned him not to do it, and others did too, but go ahead he would, and brought in the diggers. It's a while ago now, but from the day he dug out that fort, the family had no luck, no luck at all. One son got sick and never recovered; they lost what money they had; and their land went from bad to worse. He should never have interfered with that place. You're not meant to.'

Eileen points to a nearby hill, where a man deliberately removed a fairy fort from the farm he had bought a few years previously. 'He was told not to, warned of the consequences, but he was from the city and wouldn't listen. Wasn't he dead within the year?'

Your misfortune just might be reversed if you are quick enough to undo the fault. A story is told of a fairy fort where the farmer unwisely cut a bush from it to fence a gap. He was instantly struck blind, but on hastily having the bush put back in place, his sight was restored.

In Clarecastle, Co. Clare, some of the oldest inhabitants well remember the man who went to root out the bushes in the fort. A blackberry thorn pierced his eye and he lost his sight completely. Another man was wounded when a thorn pierced the sole of a strong leather boot and entered his foot. He was lame for the rest of his life.

A man who deliberately cut down all the trees around a ráth was asking for trouble, as was recalled in Co. Kildare:

There is a Ráth in Mr Price's field near Robertstown and a man named William Price who owned the field at that time went out one day and cut down the trees on the Ráth so that he could plough the field. After that one of his arms got paralysed and he shivered until he died.

A similar story comes from Westmeath:

Bad luck befell a man by the name of Cristy Dalton of Rathnugent for cutting down a tree in a fort about three years ago. All his lambs died the next year. It is said that if you cut a bush in a fort you will have bad luck the whole year.

And from Gurteen, Co. Galway, comes a similar warning message:

Hawthorn in full bloom.

Long ago there was a man building a wall around a field near the fort in Greally's field, and a fairy came out of the fort and struck him with a brush and he never built the wall since.

One Galway schoolchild of the 1930s was very clear on what a fairy lios or fort was, and what should not be attempted there:

1. There is a very old lios, in the village of Cragane. It is said it is there since the time of the Fenians [Fianna].
2. It is round in shape, and there is an old ditch of clay built around.
3. There is also an old hawthorn tree growing inside the ditch.
4. It is said that the 'daoine maithe' lives in them. It is also said that they sweep living people into those places and leave others in their places.

5. Lights are often seen and music heard inside them.

6. Old people say that there are a lot of caves under these Lioses.

7. Nobody ever digs or ploughs them.

8. Once a man dug an old lios in order to straighten the field, and all his cattle died.

WHERE AM I AT ALL?

The meascán maraíocht is a very peculiar experience, best described as a confused condition which can descend without warning on someone passing a fort or other 'gentle' place. It occurs most often at night. The unfortunate victim is suddenly quite unable to tell which way to go or how to get home.

Now, the cynical among you might well suggest that this has more to do with over-indulgence at the local pub beforehand, but there are many recorded instances that suggest otherwise. The Gearagh in West Cork, a rare example of an ancient alluvial forest, is known to be one place where this occurs. It has a maze of winding tracks and when the meascán maraíocht descends on a hiker, fisherman or dog walker, they suddenly find they cannot discover their way out. Traditionally, this was a very useful phenomenon for the poitín makers who distilled their powerful brew on the Gearagh's many tiny islands. If customs officers came hunting, the confusing mist could descend on them and give the lads time to get away.

Here is a slightly unusual example from Co. Cavan, in which a horse assists the victim to find himself (a case of a helping hoof?):

Tracks through the Gearagh
may send you astray if
Themselves wish it.

There is an old fort in Mr Patrick McGoldrick's land in Drumbarlum. One night, Mr John Fitzpatrick of Teemore was passing by the fort when suddenly a river sprang up in front of him. No matter what way he turned, the river still kept in front of him. He was forced to remain at the fort until morning. He then followed a pony and it led him out of the fort.

Another example of meascán maraíocht demonstrates the actual delight Themselves can take in leading us poor humans astray:

Near Ballyshannon in the townland of Creevy, there is a very big fort on the top of a high hill. Lights were seen about this fort and fairies were seen dancing round it. Churning and the sound of music and singing were often heard in it. These fairies have taken people and kept them walking about the fields all night. Then when they got home, someone behind them would laugh …

Should the meascán maraíocht choose to envelop you when you have ventured closer than you should to a fairy fort or other 'gentle' place, and you cannot, try as you will, find your escape route, one tried and tested remedy is to take off your coat and turn it inside out. That, apparently, confuses the mischief-making spirits into thinking you are somebody else, and they release you from the spell. This counter-charm can be used in several different situations when you feel you are being teased by unknown spirits, whether you are near a lios or not.

Is it the mist or the meascán maraíocht?

Here is an example from Co. Monaghan:

Andy Mc Enaney was coming of his céidlidhe one night. It was very late and he came across the fort for a near cut. As he was coming past it, a big cat came dashing from the bushes and would not let him by. He made three attempts to catch the cat, but he did not succeed. He found himself very weak, but still tried to rush home. No matter where he went he could get no way out of the field. He took off his coat and turned it inside out. He then did the same with his cap: he could see the gap quite plain now. He promised he would never go by a fort again.

This writer heard a genuine account from the very man who experienced it. We were sitting near each other in the same café and got chatting. When he recounted the tale, you could not doubt from the tremor in his voice that he still felt the fear.

I had this field I'd never made use of, down by the river beyond, and I decided one fine night to go down and turn it over with the plough. It was dark when I got there, but there was a moon so I went ahead. All of a sudden, this great flock of birds – I couldn't tell if they were geese or swans – came flying in and all around me until I couldn't see beyond them. Then the tractor stopped and I couldn't get it going again. The birds disappeared at last, and I thought I'd better head for home. But would you believe it, I couldn't find the way out of that field? I went round and round and there wasn't a gate, although there must have been, since I came in that way. I can tell you I was shaking, and thought I was there for the night, but then I heard the clock in the village beyond strike midnight, and with that I could see the gap in the wall, and was able to escape.

Strange enough, but it gets stranger. I was recounting this story to an elderly lady a week or so later, and she immediately commented:

Wouldn't surprise me at all. That's the field with the old ráth in it. And one time the gypsies camped right up next to it, lit their fires and everything. And in the middle of the night didn't the river rise and sweep them all away?

'All of a sudden this great flock of birds came flying in and all around me until I couldn't see beyond them.'

Now that coincidence of stories coming so close upon one another definitely induced a shiver.

Con, an expert in the life of bats and their habitats, tells a curious tale of a recent experience.

I went up to this fairy fort towards dusk to measure the place and get some idea of what was growing there – if it was likely to house bats. I had a volunteer with me to carry the poles and things. Well, I was clumsy clambering in and happened to break a branch of a hawthorn bush. I was sorry for that, and felt like apologising to the bush, but got on with the job instead. We stood inside the fort and sighted the other side, straight across.

Then we started walking directly towards that point, to get the exact width. I was checking all the time on the compass to make sure I was going in a straight line. When we got there, I climbed up on the bank, and there was the hawthorn branch I had broken off on my way in. We were back where we had arrived! Somehow that place had skewed the equipment, thrown my compass entirely out, and brought us back to where we started. This time I did apologise, both to the bush and to the fort itself, and we made off fairly quickly.

In the northern counties, this leading-astray trick by Themselves is known as the fóidín meara, or fóidín marbh, and the cure is the same as they follow in the south:

A mountain hawthorn.

When people take the fóidín meara they turn their coats inside out and they become all right.

The 'Foidin Marbh' is a sod of ground and if you stand on it at night, you will be unable to find your way – lifted as it is called. If you take off your coat and turn it you will be alright.

This idea of the fóidín marbh as a particular piece of ground rather than a floating spell can be linked to the belief that there are places where you may encounter the Féar Gorta or Hungry Grass. This is said to grow where people died of starvation during different famines (the Great Famine of the 1840s, alas, was only one of many). If you walk on it, you are immediately struck with a deadly faintness.

It is the name often given to the terrible hunger which often strikes people when going on a journey if they step on the fóidín marbh. A little crumb of oaten bread taken is the best cure for féar gorta.

Here is a story of the fóidín meara with a less happy ending:

One evening a girl from our place was going to a wake and she fell asleep while she was walking. She walked over water and she was not a bit wet. She kept walking until morning. As soon as the sun shone in the morning, she woke and went to the nearest house. There she was told that she was six miles from her own home. She was shivering when she woke and she was put to bed and she never left it until she died.

Strange things can happen at sunset.

Themselves can organise the weather to work against you too. One man who habitually used to make his way home at night past a fairy fort was cautioned by friends that it was unwise so to do, and he would be sorry, but he ignored their warnings. One fine, calm night, as he was crossing by the fort, something began to strike the ground around him and a storm began to rage. He hurried home and escaped unhurt, but he never went that way again by night.

You might also need to be wary if a seemingly innocent stone falls in your path from a bank. A strange story from Barefield, near Ennis in Co. Clare, concerns two young men returning from a dance:

They crossed through a fort on their way home and went out a stile at the other side. Pat went first and when he was halfway through the next field he missed his companion. He went back and found him on the ground and a small stone on his breast and he was unable to rise. The stone appeared to be very small, but he was hardly able to lift if off the other man it was so heavy. When the stone was gone off his breast he got up and they both got home unhurt.

A man who deliberately set out against all advice to level the ráth on his land did not get off so lightly as that homegoing pair: the man himself went crazy; his wife fell in the yard one day, and broke her leg; and the man who worked for them got an injury to one of his eyes, which later caused blindness.

Instances of blood appearing on a hatchet being used to cut a tree in a ráth, or on the sods being turned by a plough, are many. Most farmers take heed of such a warning and desist from their clearly inadvisable project, as in this case from Co. Limerick:

Lisnafulla fort, it is said, was about to be tilled, for it contains an acre of ground. The ploughman and horses were just starting and had turned up the opening sod when spots of blood were observed on the upturned sod. The ploughman stopped his horses and folded over the sod and that's how it lies to this day.

Up at Glasbolly in Donegal, where locals often heard music coming from a fairy fort at night, the unwise landowner decided to cut a scíóg or fairy bush from it.

Looking at his axe after the first slash, he saw that it was drip-
ping blood. Of course he stopped cutting, but that night some of
his best cattle died.

A lios near the cricket field in Kilrush, Co. Clare, was ploughed by another unbeliever, who died shortly afterwards 'of a terrible disease'. A similar story from nearby Burrane claimed that the offender died 'the very next day', and all the ploughing he had done 'came together again as if it had never been dug'.

A very definite warning against such interference comes from Monaghan:

Richard Lundy, a wealthy man who lived in Ardnagh, knocked
down Ardnagh fort. While he was labouring at it his two horses
fell dead, and all his stock died that year. His daughter lost her
sight, and shortly after the name of Lundy was not in Ardnagh.

One Co. Clare landowner learned abruptly to take heed of local advice. He was eager to introduce the latest farming methods and to improve the fields on his estate near Cloonlara. Close to the route known as Cromwell's Old Road, he found there was a fairy fort right in the middle of a large field. Shaking his head at such untidiness, he ordered all its surrounding hawthorn trees to be rooted up and the ráth itself levelled. His workmen were, naturally enough, very reluctant to do so, but had little choice but to obey.

Hardly had they set to work on the first big hawthorn tree when a messenger came in haste to tell the landowner that his daughter was dying. She had been playing in the yard with

This fairy tree will not be moved.

her dogs when she was raised up, apparently by an unseen force, and dashed against the road, suffering concussion and a broken arm.

Work immediately ceased, and the daughter, fortunately, recovered slowly over some weeks. Although the field did go on to be tilled afterwards, the fort was carefully avoided from then on.

It is worth noting that, as in this story, in most cases it is the instigator of the project who is punished and not those who, often reluctantly, carry it out for him. The Good People are nothing if not fair-minded. Here is an example of that, this time from the delightfully named Skeheenarenky (Sceichín na Rince, the Little Thorn Bush of the Dancing, a name which certainly carries distinct echoes of the Otherworld), in Co. Tipperary. In this instance, the man who ordered the work is only looking on:

Old Jim Curtain's uncle named Casey hired a man from Mitchelstown to dig a Lios. While the man was digging Casey was crippled. He was in bed for some time. He was brought one day to Sheila Rodey's and placed on a height where he had a good view of the races which were to take place. He was not long seated on there when he was thrown down the hill; and he never left his bed until he died.

It must surely be the most terrifying of experiences to find yourself trapped in a ráth and unable to get out. Mairéad Gordon recorded hearing of just such an experience:

This is a story which my mother heard from her father. It was about himself and another man who went out minding sheep in Stone Park and they had a little dog named Tiny with them. There was a fort in the field and the dog who ran on before them stopped at it and began to sneeze as they thought.
There was a hole on the top of the hill and they went into it. When they went in they heard some noise. They could not get

out when they went in, even though they saw many places at which they thought they could get out. When daylight came they saw a great lot of mud there. When they got home they found that the dog had been beaten by some fairies or somebody and he did not wake for several days.

As we were finalising this book for publication, we met a postman near the Kerry border. (Postmen are great for gathering up the old legends and stories as they go around the countryside from farm to cottage, laneway to laneway.) Told of what we were working on, he enthusiastically recounted several tales of ill luck following those who were foolish enough to interfere with fairy forts. Here is just one:

And there were these two brothers who dug up several of them – wouldn't listen to reason, went right ahead and levelled them to the ground. Well, they were both lost in the river not long after, when their car went off the road. That's what you get when you do something so foolish.

Can we really discount every one of these eerie (if not downright frightening) occurrences as simply coincidence? One feels even that such deliberate refusal to believe might be flying in the face of – of what? Divine retribution perhaps?

Here is a genuine experience of our own, while working on this book: We went out into north Cork to photograph a particular ráth on a narrow back road. We didn't climb into it (it was very overgrown), but went round the outside to try to get different shots. Suddenly, Richard said his camera batteries had gone completely dead. He switched to the spares, only to find they were inexplicably dead too. Naturally, as a professional, he always makes sure they are fully charged whenever he goes out on a job. This time there wasn't a spark in them.

We made our way back to the car, wondering how this had happened. And the car wouldn't start. At all. We tried everything, but no luck. While waiting for roadside assistance, two different farmers passed by on their tractors and, as is the kindly way in the countryside, stopped to offer help. Both, on hearing that we had been trying to record the ráth, said effectively, 'Well, that's what you get for interfering with Themselves.' The mechanic who turned up hours later (it was a very remote laneway) said exactly the same thing.

What was actually wrong with the car, you ask? The mechanic couldn't tell. He tried this, tried that, unplugged everything and plugged it all in again, rang the head office for advice … Eventually, the Good People relented, and it started. We were glad to get home.

Odd enough, but curiously echoed by our O'Brien Press book designer, Emma Byrne, when we shared that story with her:

Isn't that amazing? This stuff is real! A few years ago, RTÉ did a piece with me on book cover design for the Irish Book Awards, and the cameraman that was down had been in the area previously, doing a piece on a fairy field with a local folklorist. He had a similar story about returning to his car to find the battery completely flat when it had no reason to be, and he had no end of trouble getting out of there.

I wonder with these sites – fairies or not, they are ancient, there are often ley lines. They aren't there by accident, but rather by design, so are there minerals in the soil that contribute to odd goings on? Be careful, adhere to warnings and respect the small folk whatever you do!

Sensible advice. It doesn't do to think you know better than Those who have been here since the Earth was young.

The fairy fort that stopped the car.

The Good People prefer to move about after dark

CHAPTER IV

OVERHEARD – OR EVEN GLIMPSED?

The belief that fairy forts must never be interfered with, never damaged or (the gods forfend) even removed altogether in the interests of progress, is so deeply rooted that it withstands all pressure from the grinding juggernaut of modern development. But it's more than just a belief – it is backed up by so many records of hearing strange things, even (though more rarely) actually witnessing strange and inexplicable events, that the conviction has, if anything, grown stronger over the centuries.

Doubters will always be plentiful. Many, especially those who have grown up in cities, are only too eager to explain away such happenings as mere 'coincidence' or 'imagination'. However, there are rather too many instances on record to explain away in such a convenient and thoughtless manner. It should also be stressed that these are not only old accounts or venerable stories, but real, modern-day experiences too.

'Oh, there's a place over there, beyond the hill,' one countryman says matter-of-factly. 'You'd often hear music coming from it when you'd be passing late at night. Sometimes lights too, and it couldn't be young people amusing themselves, because you couldn't get at that same fort for the thorns and the bushes.' He nods, accepting this as a normal part of life.

By far the most common among events recorded as occurring at or near a fairy fort is music. The Tuatha dé Danann placed enormous value on the power of music to affect the mind, heart and soul, and skilled harpists were placed in high positions among the nobility to reflect their importance. This, it would seem, has been continued in their Otherworld today. Hidden from our perception most of the time, it occasionally spills out into the night air just to remind us that They are there.

> *There is an old trunk of a tree by a fort, and it is hollow. Singing was heard in it, and a small stone for sharpening a scythe was found in it.*
>
> *It is said that when the people were up in the silence of the night, lights were to be seen and music heard, called the 'Ceol Sidhe'. It is said that angry cats would come out from every side of the Lios if you would go near it.*

The traditional Irish harp, of course, but also the fiddle and the pipes, are favourite instruments among Themselves. The last-named would probably not have been the bagpipe, but rather something closer to wooden Pan pipes. An archaeological excavation in Co. Wicklow in 2003 revealed a set of carefully carved yew tubes that would have fitted this use. There are many stories recorded that describe hearing this instrument, one such identifying a fairy mound near Terryglass in Tipperary:

> *[This] is always known as the Piper's Rock because, it is said, the fairy piper used to come and play his wonderful music at the dead of night, and this was followed by fairy dancing. Not far away, at Knockshegowna, the fairies were also known to dance on moonlit nights to the unearthly music created by their own musicians.*

Knockshegowna can be variously translated as 'the hill of the lios of the goddess Danu' or 'the hill of the fort of the fairy cattle'. Whichever you prefer, its Otherworld links cannot be ignored.

The music of the Good People is regarded in our world as something utterly beautiful and unforgettable, and yet, contradictorily, impossible to recall and reproduce. Remember that wonderful chapter in *The Wind in the Willows* where Rat and Mole, searching in the early dawn for the lost baby otter, find him safely asleep at the feet of the Great God Pan? They hear the most haunting music, which they try to memorise and keep in their minds, but they are unable so to do. That writing comes very close to descriptions of hearing the music of the Good People in Ireland, from the earliest records to the most recent. If you are lucky enough to hear it, you stand still and listen, because it is impossible to ignore it and walk on, such is its enchantment; but once it is gone, and you can

Knockshegowna, a veritable fairy hill.

no longer hear one elusive note, then you will find you cannot remember how it went, what the notes were – only that it was supremely beautiful.

The Daghda, the great god who stands with Danu as the head of all the Good People, is said to be possessed of a wonderful harp on which he will play the Three Magic Tunes for his people at banquets and great occasions. These tunes reflect Happiness, Sorrow and War, and each fills its listeners with all the emotions relating to that theme – great joy, agonising grief, inspirational courage to go forth and fight. From this stems the legend of the minstrel boy who goes forth with the army into a great battle, to inspire them to fight bravely. In later centuries, Irish troops would be led by a musician playing the great war pipes, but in those ancient days, it was the musical stroke of harpstrings which brought courage.

> *The minstrel boy to the wars has gone,*
> *In the ranks of death you will find him.*
> *His father's sword he has girded on,*
> *And his wild harp slung behind him.*
> (Thomas Moore, 1779–1852)

There is another story attached to that Piper's Rock in Tipperary. It seems that when the fairies came out to dance, they frightened the local cattle herds and also their owners. One brave man, Larry by name, volunteered to go out and care for the cattle on such nights. When the fairies came out, Larry played his pipes. Annoyed at such intrusion, the Good People went and told their king. He came to Larry in the form of a

Piper's Rock, where a fairy musician
has been heard playing.

large cat, trying to frighten him, but Larry kept on playing. Then the king turned into a huge white calf. The redoubtable piper jumped on the calf's back and was taken for a ride across the countryside beyond the River Shannon. Eventually, the king admitted that Larry was very brave, brought him back, and said they would not annoy the cattle any more on that hill.

It sounds as though both these tales from Piper's Rock are intermingled, but whether there was an original fairy piper, or if it is Larry's bravery that is recalled, is difficult to ascertain.

A more unusual occurrence, which one might describe as 'travelling music', is recorded from Ballaghanea in Co. Cavan. Here, haunting fairy music was first heard at rocks in a river that flows along the Mullagh road. It then moved, and was heard crossing a hill called the Round Hill, after which it travelled to all the fairy ráths in the vicinity, before dying away. Sometimes it sounded like the music of a tin whistle, and at other times like a flute, but it was agreed that it was 'so sweet that it would lift the heaviest heart'.

Did you know that certain airs (as well as the Three Magic Tunes) are said to be the property of the Good People and are not to be played or sung lightly, especially after dark? Lady Wilde writes of this in her 1888 collection *Ancient Legends of Ireland*:

It is not right, the people say, to sing or whistle at night that old air 'The Pretty Girl Milking her Cow', for it is a fairy tune and the fairies will not suffer a mortal to sing their music while they are dancing on the grass. But if a person sleeps on the rath, the music will enter into his soul and when he awakens he may sing the air he has heard in his dreams. In this way, the bards learned their songs. And they were skilled musicians, and touched the harp with a master hand so that the fairies often gathered round to listen, though invisible to mortal eyes …

Those who hear the fairy harp 'lose all memory of love or hate, and forget all things, and never more have any other sound in their ears save the soft music of the fairy harp'.

There is a reflection here of the innumerable stories telling of people who have fallen asleep in or near a fairy ráth and woken with the gift of music. Some, usually fiddlers, were said to have been taken by the Good People to play at their feasts and, if appreciated, entrusted with the Three Magic Tunes to play – although only to a deserving audience and at appropriate times. To utilise these tunes for bad purposes could only result in the worst of bad luck for the musician.

It is therefore by no means certain that becoming a guest at an Otherworld gathering will bring benefits – it could prove quite the opposite for surly or ill-mannered human guests.

It is said that Turlough O'Carolan, the legendary blind Irish harpist of the seventeenth century, used to sleep by a fairy ráth by choice on many occasions. He claimed that this was how he gained the inspiration for his utterly beautiful compositions. These are as popular today as they ever were in his lifetime, when he would travel Ireland on horseback with his harp, accepting pleading invitations wherever he went. Skilled musicians were welcome everywhere.

Old placenames are often a clue to Otherworld occurrences. A fort near Noughaval in Co. Clare is called Liskeentha (lios caointe), because it was reputed to be the source of beautiful, unexplained songs at night. It is always, but always, worth looking more closely at placenames and considering if they offer hints to a now hidden past.

The Legend of Knockgrafton, collected and retold by Crofton Croker in 1824, is well known. A poor man by the name of Lusmore had the affliction of a hump, which made him solitary and friendless. One night, he was resting by the fort of Knockgrafton in the Glen of Aherlow, Tipperary, when he heard the Good People singing. Their song went:

Dé Luain, Dé Máirt, Dé Luain, Dé Máirt, Dé Luain, Dé Máirt … (Monday, Tuesday, Monday, Tuesday, Monday, Tuesday) repeated over and over.

After listening with much enjoyment, Lusmore decided to get involved, and at the end of one repeat, swiftly interposed 'agus Dé Céadaoin' (and Wednesday). This addition gave the song a much better rhythm, and the Good People were so pleased that they magically removed his hump. Another humpback, Jack Madden, became jealous and thought he would try his luck – but didn't bother with the subtleties of phrasing and timing. Instead he just shouted out, 'Agus Déardaoin, agus Dé hAoine, agus Dé Sathairn,' (And Thursday, and Friday, and Saturday) with no style to it at all, which annoyed his listeners mightily. In revenge, they not only left his hump in place, but added Lusmore's on top of it. Moral: Don't think you can get away with poor composition when your audience is the Good People, superb musicians themselves!

Music, then, is very commonly heard from fairy forts. Now and again, though, you come across more unusual sounds –

the dragging of chains, for instance, an anvil being struck or 'the sound of churning'. These days, most of us would not be familiar with the sound made by the rhythmic turning of the wooden butter churn, but in earlier times it would have been as familiar as the crow of the cockerel or the call of the curlew.

Butter churns in Cork Butter Museum.

It's a thumping, knocking noise, and it is fascinating to imagine what might have caused such a sound inside a fairy fort, especially if there are no tracks leading to it and no apparent point of entry, as is so often the case. (You'll soon find that out for yourself when you go looking, and try to push your way through impenetrable brambles and tangled thorn trees.)

At a small fort on the hill of Cnocnaratha (the Hill of the Fairy Forts) near Ennis in Co. Clare, 'queer churning sounds like a stick hitting the walls of an underground room' are sometimes heard. Is it the Good People moving treasure through the underground passages? Fairy butter being made? One can fancy many different possibilities, but Themselves are not likely to let us into their private activities.

One Sligo farmer decided to use the fairy fort on his land to store a rick of hay. In due course, he agreed to sell some of this to another farmer, and they came by night to collect it. However, when they came near to the fort, they saw it brightly lit up and heard the noise of a crowd of men working at taking the hay away themselves. Becoming nervous, they went away without interfering. Next day, though, the hay was still there, as if nothing had happened. Perhaps the Good People wanted to remind the farmer that what was put in the fort stayed in the fort?

A landowner in Rosroe, Co. Galway, decided, against all local advice, to use stones from a fairy ráth on his land to build his new house. Once installed, though, he found no peace. Every night, there arose a racket, with the sound of breaking china, chairs being thrown about and worse. In the end, he had to abandon that property and build again further away

– without, this time, utilising stones from the fort. It is not known if he returned the original material to its proper home, but it is to be hoped that he did. Bad luck can continue if you do not remedy your first mistake.

It does make you wonder about stories that we hear from time to time of poltergeists (or playful ghosts) making householders' lives a misery. Does this in fact stem from something they have done that has annoyed the Good People? Like the untouched hay in the fairy fort that we noted above, the most appalling of crashes and apparent smashing of china is only heard, not actually carried out. When the family rushes out of bed to see what's going on, everything seems to be still in its proper place. (It is always in the middle of the night, Themselves preferring the dark hours for moving around.) Perhaps the house has been built across a fairy path (more of that in a later chapter), or it includes stones borrowed from a nearby lios. Or something else entirely. Should you ever have the misfortune to be tormented by inexplicable disturbances at night, before you call for an exorcism, examine the situation carefully first, to see if some conciliatory action on your part might end the annoyance.

This writer's father had two very good friends in childhood, the Conran twins. Identical twins are known to attract poltergeists for some reason – perhaps these playful ghosts are amused by the fact of two such similar beings? The boys lived in an old house, where quite frequently at night a poltergeist would vigorously turn the handle of a heavy old iron mangle that stood in a corner of the kitchen. (For those too young to remember a time before modern laundry facilities, the mangle squeezed the excess water out of clothes before they were hung out to dry.) But next morning, no result was to be seen from this energetic ghostly exercise. Everything remained as it had been when the family had retired to bed. Well, you couldn't expect them to do the housework, could you? 'What do you think we are, brownies or servants or something?'

All the same, it seems Themselves will make practical use of human tools and conveniences when it suits them so to do. This engaging information on Otherworld 'sewing bees' comes from Corvally in Monaghan:

There is a fort called Jones' Fort in the townland of Mullagh-croghery. Until recently fairies lived in it. There was a house opposite the fort and the fairies used to come into it. Every night after the people of the home had gone to bed, they heard the sewing machine being pulled to the middle of the floor and then in a little while they heard the sound of sewing. In the morning sometimes the machine was still in the middle of the floor, and stools and chairs were out of their accustomed places. Sometimes the fairies would borrow the measuring tape or the thimbles, but they were always returned in a night again.

Themselves can be helpful too, if so minded and if the house-holders are kindly. At a house near a ráth by Castleblayney in Co. Monaghan, the fairies came in at night and washed the dishes. They set the plates straight up on the edge of the shelf. If you lifted one off, they would all come crashing down.

The Good People definitely have a sense of humour, and enjoy teasing the human beings who venture into their domain, as this tale from Cavan shows:

In Belturbet at the top of Deanery Street, opposite the Parochial House, there is a big field with mounds and trees all round them. Some people say that these mounds are Fairy Forts. There are cattle grazing in the field. There is a story told that when a man would go into this field in the evening for the cattle his hat would be taken off his head mysteriously and placed on the grass in the middle of the field. When going over to lift the hat he could hear a number of people laughing aloud but could see no one. When he reached the spot, the hat would be gone but he could see it in another part of the field. Then he would say aloud 'Now boys, I have to go home with the cows,' and then he would find the hat back on his head.

In other recorded incidents, someone may go out near to a fairy fort with a spade or other implement, only to have it disappear and turn up a hundred yards away. Sometimes this is to express displeasure at an intended invasion, but at other times, it seems to be simply for fun.

Hearing unearthly music or other weird sounds near a fort or ráth is fairly common then in both folklore and memory, as is the experience of seeing strange moving lights, either within the lios or moving around outside it. Some witnesses aver that they have seen what appears to be communication between two different fairy forts close to one another.

In Donegal in the 1930s, a schoolboy called Bob Moore listed fairy forts in the townlands of Mullinacross, Tullywee, Tullygallon, Trummon, Mullinacole and Roscilly.

The farmer driving his cattle home may be teased by Themselves.

There is also a fort in Murvagh beside our byre. It is circular in shape and there is a large sciog bush beside it, round which the fairies dance. The people would not cut down the sciog bush because they thought it would bring bad luck to them. It is said that from one fort, another can be seen and from these the fairies signalled one to another, and it is also said that there are tunnels from one to another and when they were attacked they escaped to the next fort.

And apparently there was a lios just outside Ennis on the road to Gort, where every night, strange lights were seen flashing. The construction of a new hospital made its removal inevitable, but who knows, perhaps those lights flash still in the wee small hours?

Seeing actual beings or events is rarer. It does occur, though. In Co. Clare, there is a fort with a central mound of earth upon which many fairies are claimed to have been seen dancing and singing. At a fairy mound near Allenwood in Co. Kildare, a strange phenomenon has often been seen, according to local folklore:

Every night something with showers of sparks falling from it rises in Mr Quinn's bottoms [i.e. the lower part of Quinn's field] and runs along the black boreen and goes down the hole in the top of the Crocán Hill. I saw the lighted object myself. One time some people tried to raise gravel in the Crocán Hill but the little people stopped them, and no-one ever tried to get gravel since. Music is also heard in this rath.

And this story comes from Mayo:

There is a fairy bush east of our house on the road side. It is a white thorn bush. People can see lights of many colours jumping around that bush at about twelve o'clock.

One time a man passed that bush when he was coming from town and he saw a small man sitting on the bush. He walked quickly passing the bush and the man disappeared. When he looked behind he saw a few lights like candles running across the road after one another. He walked quickly home that night and he is afraid passing that bush ever since. The bush is still there.

Another typical one from Athlone:

At twelve o'clock in the night fairies can be seen marching round the fort. There is not a big distance between the two forts and late at night lights can be seen going from one to another.

At the lios na sídeóg, or fairy fort, near Cartron in Sligo, the fairies can be seen dancing before midnight, but after that, the entire lios disappears for two hours. This could be an instance of the Otherworld host travelling on to dance or feast at another fort, and concealing their movement by bringing down a thick mist or fog. The Tuatha dé Danann were expert in the old magic, and could conjure up an enveloping cloud to influence the course of a battle or an invasion whenever needed. They did this in fact when the Celts first invaded, but unfortunately the leader of the invaders, Amergin by name, was also knowledgeable in the old magic and was able to counteract it by chanting a powerful spell of his own.

It is still held today that if the top of a mountain or hill is covered with mist or cloud, then the Good People are on their way to some exciting event elsewhere and don't wish you to witness their journey. Shehy Mountain near Inchigeela in Co. Cork is a well-known example. If you can see the pointed top clearly, Themselves are staying home. If the top is wreathed in thick cloud, then they are on the move.

Similarly, if you see a sudden whirling of leaves along the road, it's the sidhe gaoithe, or fairy wind, showing that the Good People are passing by. It is considered advisable to

Above: Shehy Mountain showing its summit – the fairies are staying home.

Below: Shehy Mountain with mist, showing Themselves are on the move.

raise your hat or bow your head when you witness the fairy wind, acknowledging Their passing.

In ancient times there were fairies in Ireland and there are still fairy breezes. While the people were out in the fields making hay a breeze would come and take the hay off the ground and take it up in the air. They called this a fairy breeze. One day I was out in the field and I heard a noise coming through the bushes. The stalks were taken off the drills and the sheaves of oats were taken about a half mile away from the field. The breeze lasted about three minutes.

Another story from that ráth near Cartron concerns two men returning from the day's work with their horses and carts. They saw distant lights and knew they came from the fort. As it happened, they had no matches to get their pipes going, and one said bravely, 'If only I had one of those lights for my pipe.' Upon that, the entire road lit up brilliantly before them. Discretion being the better part of valour, they did not wait to take advantage of the generously offered illumination, but headed for home as fast as they could.

Drumullen Fort in Co. Clare is the background for a really eerie experience recounted in the 1930s. An old man and his wife were setting out for Limerick market with a load of butter and eggs on their donkey cart. In the early hours of the morning, they saw an actual ship crossing Rathluby Lake from the direction of the fort. Near a healing spring known as Gloucester's Well, the ship left the lake and sailed up the road towards Ballyroughan. Needless to say, the couple were

terrified and, forgoing any idea of going to market, turned hastily for home. It's hard to find a rational explanation for such a vision. An image from an earlier time, when waterways took different routes? An Otherworld boat, like that of Manannán mac Lir, which can travel over land and sea with equal facility? If only one person had seen it, there would be reasonable grounds for doubt, but two witnesses?

Also in Co. Clare, there are several instances of a ghostly figure being seen near a ráth called Lissahan. One first looked like a statue, but then grew larger and larger and finally went up into the clouds. Another was a strange man appearing to walk slowly alongside a fast-moving pony and trap, but actually drawing ahead of it. A lady and gentleman, arms linked, are sometimes seen late at night, strolling up and down by the fairy fort near Castlegal in Sligo, accompanied by two big dogs. A small woman dressed in black has also been seen at the same location, though less frequently.

One of the strangest tales comes from Tipperary. Two men were headed to the fair in Thurles early one morning and were passing a well-known ráth when, to their horror, a funeral came out, with some 300 carriages following the hearse. Two Otherworld men were in each car, except the last, in which there was one very old patriarch with a long, white beard, hanging right down to his feet. Standing upright, he nodded to the two men as the procession passed. 'The men did not go to the fair that day,' said the girl who recounted this story. 'They went home.' Well yes, most of us would after an experience like that.

Great black dogs have been recorded in and around fairy forts, as well as wild-eyed cats of enormous size and even white fairy horses. The cats often have speech and warn the intruder not to interfere. At Lios na gCat in Co. Cavan, and Cathair na gCat in Kerry, though, you might well encounter packs of huge black cats, who have the reputation of killing and eating

anyone who comes too close. The spirit dogs will often follow a passer-by until he is able to find a stream to cross, as these Otherworld animals will not enter flowing water.

Con, the bat expert whom we quoted in the last chapter as having been cunningly led astray by Themselves, had another odd experience when he was checking out a ráth on a hill:

I went further up the hillside to get a view from above, and looked down. I noticed several rather nice ponies ambling around the fort while I was doing this. Then I came down again and didn't think about them until I was back by the car. A farmer came by and I asked him who owned those fine animals. He looked surprised and said there were no ponies there, never had been. It wasn't a suitable place for them. I looked up and around, and sure enough, there were no horses to be seen, nor any trace of them in the surrounding fields. Yet I had seen them clearly enough from the top of the hill. Were they an echo of the past? Ponies belonging to those who lived in the fairy fort long ago? I still don't know, and it still puzzles me.

One of the most endearing records of Otherworld animal sightings is of a belligerent fairy sow, reputed to live in a lios near Inniscarra in Co. Cork. She would have been more of the wild boar type than the modern placid farm animal, as these were plentiful in older times. Apparently, this tough porcine resented any intruders and would viciously pelt them with stones. Can't you just picture the massive porker, her chin thrust out in anger, her small eyes boring into visitors as she seizes her ammunition with a cloven hoof and aims these sharp missiles all too accurately? And with fairy power too! Off-putting in the extreme to any intending explorer, one would think. Even the toughest of hunting dogs would consider his alternative options or remember an urgent appointment elsewhere.

If you are out and about near a lios or ráth yourself late at night, and suddenly think you hear something strange or even glimpse an unexpected movement, don't dismiss it as tiredness or imagination. Stand still, listen and look hard. You never know what you might experience.

A small white cow with red ears could well be a fairy animal.

Chapter V

Who Are the Good People?

We mentioned this in Chapter II, but it's worth saying again: Forget any notions of 'fairies' that you might have garnered in childhood – tiny, sparkly creatures with gossamer wings, flitting here and there, popping up on the pantomime stage. Or indeed little brownies or goblins, set on either doing good or making mischief. Ireland's Good People are quite another kind of being. They are spirits of nature, gods of our most ancient beliefs. They therefore command huge respect. Although we talk of 'fairy forts', those who are believed to inhabit these domains are called variously the Good People, Themselves, the Gentry or the Other Crowd. It is a very old tradition that you do not speak of such beings by their actual name, as this would show disrespect and possibly invite reprimand or punishment.

They are often identified as the Tuatha dé Danann, or the People of Danu (she is the supreme earth mother or nature goddess of Ireland). They came to Ireland long ago, it is said, in a great mist. Some legends hold that they originated in the far North, possibly shamans from the Norselands or Russia. Other intriguing tales link them to southern lands, and indeed the Lebor Gabhala, the Book of Invasions, states that our very first settler was a princess, Cessair by name, who fled with her followers from the rising seas and consequent inundations of her native land in the Aegean. The Book of Invasions links this to the Deluge and Noah, but the factual history of a great flooding (almost certainly caused by the melting of ice caps) is, fascinatingly, in there too:

> *This is the reason for her coming, fleeing from the Flood, for Noe said until them: Rise, said he [and go] to the western edge of the world; perchance the Flood may not reach it. The crew of three ships arrived at Dun na Rarc in the territory of Corco Duibhne.*

Recent researches have suggested that it is within this legend of the Great Flood that the true history of Atlantis lies. Once a great kingdom in the Aegean, much of it disappeared below the rising seas, leaving only the highest points visible today as multiple islands of Greece. Was Cessair a princess of legendary Atlantis, and did she bring the ancient knowledge and magical skills of that island with her to Ireland?

Whether it was Atlanteans or northern shamans, they are said to have ritually burned the boats in which they arrived, to declare their intention of living here forever. As indeed they have done, since the belief is strong that they are a vibrant magical presence in the Ireland of today. The many fairy ráths, dúns and lios that dot our countryside are still held to be visible evidence of their homes.

Their greatest enemies at first were the Fomorians, a tribe of savage piratical raiders. From their bases on offshore islands, they came ashore to attack, kill and carry off food and slaves. These pirates were finally defeated by the Tuatha dé Danann at the Second Battle of Moytura.

Inhabiting this land, therefore, long before the Celts set sail from northern Spain to reach our coast, the Tuatha dé Danann fought long and hard to defend their land when these later, determined invaders arrived. Only in the last resort did they agree to leave the visible ground to the warlike conquerors, withdrawing into the ground beneath their fairy mounds and forts, there to continue their magical lifestyle forever. In so doing, they became, in effect, a pantheon of gods in their own right, taking on many of the attributes of the ancient spirits.

Factually speaking, that there were such people as the Tuatha here before the coming of the Celts is self-evident. Since they left such incredible monuments, clearly they were a very advanced race: learned, skilled, easily able to conceive and carry out huge projects that would be a challenge even today. Although the Tuatha dé Danann were not of an age that left written records, they did bequeath an amazing heritage in both the countless fairy forts still to be seen everywhere, and in stone monuments like those of Brú na Bóinne, which show that their builders were possessed of very advanced skills and knowledge. These ancient megaliths are far older than Stonehenge, older even than the Egyptian Pyramids, dating from over 5,000 years ago. Small wonder then that the incoming

Celts gazed on them with wonderment and assumed that they must have been created by the gods themselves.

The oldest records state firmly that these early people of Ireland also possessed many magical skills, learned in their former homes, whether in the Northlands or Greece, and that they used these to create a wonderful world around them, as well as to discourage raiders or invaders. For instance, it was an easy task for the Tuatha to raise a high wind, a violent storm or a dense fog that would hinder any planned attack.

In everyday life, however, they led a joyous existence. Always described as tall, bright-haired and happy, they were fond of music, song and dancing; constantly visiting each other's kingdoms to exchange gifts and arrange marriages. In fact, they were a complete contrast to the dark, aggressive Celts, who had long known of this fertile green island in the far west and came determined to conquer whoever lived there and take these rich lands for themselves.

Today, most would consider typical Irish looks to be dark-haired and dark-eyed ('eyes put in with a smutty finger' is the classic description), but that in fact applies to those of Celtic blood. Anyone tracing their descent to the earlier peoples is more likely to be fair-haired and blue-eyed. Whether from the Norselands, then, or southernmost Greece, these Tuatha dé Danann certainly came from lands where music, crafts and feasting were held in high regard, and these qualities they brought with them to Ireland. Those characteristics of Irish life are still as strong as ever.

Of course, the Celts brought their own gods and beliefs with them. Some of these became slowly assimilated into the earlier pantheon, but the older ones remained and are firmly in situ to this day. A glance at some of the principal deities is appropriate, starting with the female side, since women were esteemed very highly in older Ireland, a desirable state that we have still not quite returned to today.

GODDESSES OF THE OTHERWORLD

Danu is the first and earliest, the earth mother, goddess of all the land and of nature itself. Also known as Áine or Anu, she holds the land of Ireland in her especial care. Her veneration is universal throughout the country, even if sometimes it has been overlaid with the doctrines of much later invaders, like the Church of Rome, which by then was becoming more and more male-dominated and took care to demote goddesses into minor figures wherever they found them.

An important fact: in marked contrast to later traditions, ancient Ireland believed instinctively in the power of women as well as (if not more than) men, and recognised the need to balance male and female attributes to ensure the good of all. Our old Brehon laws upheld these beliefs strongly, and, as this writer has shown elsewhere [*Brehon Laws: The Ancient Wisdom of Ireland*, O'Brien Press, 2020], women enjoyed much more equality with men than they have yet obtained today, advanced though we may consider ourselves to be. There are therefore as many female gods among the Tuatha dé Danann as there are male.

You will find visible evidence of the continuing worship of Danu wherever you travel, in the grottoes and shrines that dot the countryside. Today these are ostensibly dedicated to Mary, the mother of Jesus Christ, and the usual layout is of the

apparition that appeared at Lourdes in the Pyrenees, at Knock in Co. Mayo and at several other locations in the late nineteenth century – i.e. two statues, one raised, the other kneeling below, both formed very much in the Italian style, with idealised faces of adoration. Behind that, however, lie millennia of deep-seated belief in and veneration of the mother goddess who looks after the well-being of the land – its fertility, its crops, its people, all the things that make life possible. May Day celebrations are a particular example of this continuing belief, with flowers, processions, decoration of wells and springs and more, all greeting the mother figure with joy and honour at the beginning of summer. Ireland has always depended on the fertility of its land, the ability to raise crops and livestock to feed its people, as well as trade with other countries. Naturally enough, then, the instinctive reaching toward a benevolent earth goddess who sees to these things like a caring mother.

The Paps of Danu, two softly rounded mountains, rise into the sky above the road to Killarney on the Cork/Kerry border. Huge examples of the fairy mounds where the Good People live, they also represent the goddess in her most visible form, promising comfort and safety to all her people. Nestled between the Paps is the Cathair, an ancient stone fort where on 1 May every year, hundreds gather to pay homage and to collect water from the sacred well for their livestock and pets. This well is unusual in that the water from this source is to be used for the wellbeing of animals only, not for humans, who can resort to other wells elsewhere – further evidence of the care Danu extends to all her domain. Celebrations are also held on other hills, notably Cnoc Áine (Knockainey) in Co. Limerick where at midnight on Midsummer Eve bundles of straw were traditionally carried up to the top of the hill and set alight to honour the goddess. Later the ashes would be spread through the fields to ensure fertility in the year ahead.

With time, while Danu remained (and still remains) the overall earth mother, present everywhere and overseeing all, she also devolved into the tripartite goddess form so beloved in Irish mythology (a belief borrowed and used strongly by the much later Roman Church). These three forms are Brigit, the Cailleach and the Morrigan or Bean Sídhe. In other cultures, you will find these described as Maiden, Crone and Mother, but in Ireland they could be more accurately identified as Warmth, Wisdom and Warning.

Brigit (also called Brigid, Bríd, Bride and Bridget) is the maiden who has particular responsibility for spring and fertility – for life itself. Crops, young animals and crafts in all their forms are her especial care. Imbolc, on 1 February, is recognised as her special day, when lambs are beginning to be born and ewes are coming back into milk, thus ending the privations of winter. Brigit's Cross, an artefact made of woven rushes, is still made today to mark the beginning of spring. It is not in fact a cross, but an emblem of the spring – the very old swastika design, which dates from about 6,000 years ago and probably originated in Indian rock and cave paintings. Representing goodness and happiness, it is probably the oldest emblem drawn or made by humans, and it is heartening to see it still being woven industriously by schoolchildren today, even if they do it under the auspices of a much later religion.

That is because Brigit had a rough time at the hands of the Roman Church, which, by the time it reached Ireland, was becoming aggressively male-dominated. A goddess who was worshipped as the giver of life, good crops, healthy animals and children was anathema to this religion, which was by then very much altered from the simple tenets of human love preached by its founder. Brigit, clearly, had to be removed. However, that turned out not to be possible. Her worship was so entrenched that they simply couldn't stamp it out. And so the Church undertook their usual Plan B – turn her into something else, something more acceptable to their doctrine.

Brigit was recreated as Saint Brigid, a gentle, unassuming, interceding figure, plucking nervously at the cloak of an all-powerful male god. Much as the statues in today's grottoes do, in fact, whereas their original figures would have stormed into action on their own account, fighting their own battles and making their own decisions.

Ireland's goddesses are mighty and powerful in their own right, which should always be remembered when dealing with them. Brigit was gentle when gentleness was required, merciless when dealing with wrongful deeds or lack of care for those she cherished. She has continued to be venerated, in both her original and invented personas, and the name Brigit, in all its forms (Brigid, Bríd, Breda, etc.), is still one of the most popular in Ireland today. Rivers are also named for her, and there are one or two River Brides in every county.

(As an interesting side note, the Christian St Brigid was actually removed from the saints' calendar by Pope Paul VI as recently as 1969, because it was considered that there was insufficient contemporary documentary evidence to prove her existence. One might wonder how much Brigit the goddess had to do with that.)

The Cailleach is an ancient figure who encapsulates the wisdom and experience of Danu. She is guardian of the old magic, the sacred knowledge. While Brigit rules the summer, the dark winter months are the province of the Cailleach, who holds the secrets of childbirth, marriage, healing, death and rebirth. She watches and observes, and will sometimes, if approached respectfully and humbly, give advice or guidance. However, this is almost always in mystical utterings, very difficult to understand or apply. But within this is its own wisdom – nothing worthwhile in this world is ever easy or simple. Her role has been carried on throughout our history by the wise women of every generation – those who have gathered knowledge of herbs and plants, can treat illnesses and problems and are still consulted by anyone who has need of the ancient ways of dealing with life's issues. In other countries, such wise women have been harshly treated or dismissed as foolish, but in Ireland they still believe in the power of the crone or Cailleach, and continue to visit those who continue this tradition for advice or guidance.

The traditional image of a hideous old hag at her cauldron is one promoted by male-dominated religions. In seeking to overthrow the female side of balanced power, this effectively demonises these guardians of the old ways, turning them into figures to be feared, hated and persecuted, rather than venerated for their knowledge as they always should be.

You will find the Old One's name and even her person commemorated all over the country in place names like Leabacallee (the Bed of the Cailleach), Sliabh na Caillí (Mountain of the Cailleach) and Ceann Caillí (Hag's Head). Most dramatically, she is acknowledged in the Cailleach Beara, a great stone situated at Coulagh Bay on the Beara Peninsula in West Cork. Here believers still come in great numbers to leave gifts and tokens, hoping for answers to their whispered wishes. The Cailleach is married to the great god of the sea, Manannán Mac Lir, so between them they rule both land and water. The vast stone sits staring out to sea, watching always for her sea-god husband. It may be described off-handedly by geologists as a 'glacial erratic', but you have only to see the small offerings heaped around it and tucked into its crevices to realise that for many it conveys enormous power and wisdom. You can feel these qualities even as you stand by her side.

The Morrigan (Mór Rígan, or Great Queen), on the other hand, is more of an aggressive goddess than a gentle one.

The Cailleach Beara, married to the sea god Manannán Mac Lir.

Power she certainly possesses – in spades, as the expression would have it. Her more familiar name is of course the banshee (bean sidhe, or woman of the Otherworld), who is said to utter the caoine or death lament aloud (usually late at night) when the end is nigh for someone. She is often heard near fairy forts or mounds, but also across the open countryside.

There are those who hold that she will only give the caoine for a member of a family with an O or Mac surname – that is, 'daughter of' or 'son of' and thus from an old Irish clan. However, with constant intermarriage, it must be hard for her to be sure these days. Certainly, the evidence of those who have heard the banshee is that it can be for anyone – that is, as long as the wailing goddess herself considers that person to be of sufficient importance. And we do not have access to her private files on that most

secret knowledge. All we do know is that the person about to pass on never hears the cry, only those who are related or involved in some way.

In her warlike aspect as the Morrigan of ancient times, she was fierce, wild, demanding, implacable. She it was who oversaw and manipulated every famous battle of ancient Ireland, championing one side or the other as she perceived the rights and wrongs of the dispute, or indeed as the humour took her. She often took on the guise of a huge black raven, flying over the chaos and bloodshed, and she still appears today as a harshly croaking raven, uttering warnings from a high point to those who can understand her words. Next time you pass a ráth or lios and see a raven perched on a thorn tree atop the bank, it might be a good thing to bow or curtsey in acknowledgement and respect.

Belief in the banshee is exceptionally strong even in modern-day Ireland. This goddess has effortlessly maintained her position in our world over thousands of years, travelling down quite unchanged since prehistory, resisting all attempts to turn her into something gentler, kinder, more acceptable. Wherever you go and whoever you ask, everyone, old or young, will have heard of her, and quite often will be able to tell you a frightening story or two. Some (on being reassured that you are not just teasing them) will admit to having heard or even seen her, though the latter is rare indeed.

Helena, who grew up on the Connemara coast, where the old ways and old beliefs are still strong, says she has heard the banshee a few times. The cry is unlike anything else, unmistakeable: 'If you were to ask me to imitate it now, I couldn't. There isn't any way you could. It's just not of this world.'

She recalls her grandmother putting her head up sharply to listen, and then saying to her granddaughter, "Look out the window quick and you will see the flash of light passing that ruined wall there." I did, and saw it, and then the cry came again. "Ah," said my granny, "there's someone died below in the village." It wasn't twenty minutes later the phone rang to tell us of the death.'

The wailing lament of the banshee is unearthly, far-reaching and freezing to the blood when heard echoing on the wind across bogland or over a wild mountainside, as this tale from Co. Donegal demonstrates:

It always foretold the death of some person. I had a strange personal experience in this connection. One night at the time of the big flu epidemic, my sister and I went out at ten o'clock to get some turf to 'rake the fire'. Suddenly we heard a most unearthly cry. It started about a mile away from us and ran along the ground for about half a mile. Then it began to ascend and went up, up, up, getting fainter as it went until it died away in the sky. We never heard anything so weird and concluded that it must be the banshee. We went home and told our people that we heard a banshee. They laughed at us. It happened that our next-door neighbour, Mrs D – whose maiden name was Gallagher – took the flu that night and was dead that day week.

City dwellers, and those who find reassurance in ascribing mundane explanations to inexplicable happenings, have often claimed that it is 'simply' the call of a fox or the screech of a barn owl. As if it were that simple! Presumably they do not take into account the wide experience of country dwellers in every sound, call, croak or chirp that may be encountered throughout the day or night. They are well able to distinguish the normal from the unearthly.

''Twas like a cat, only no cat I ever heard.'

'It would put you in mind of a vixen and she screeching, but a vixen will stop and listen for the dog fox every now and then. This went on and on and on, the way no animal could do.'

As John Joe, a wise old folklorist living on the very slopes of the Paps of Danu, says, thumping the table: 'Do you not understand what I'm telling you? If you are meant to hear it, then hear it you will!'

'My father always claimed he heard her one night, when he was coming home,' admits Denis, a supermarket manager. 'He said it made his hair stand on end.'

The banshee is often heard near old ruins.

Is it ever heard in cities? Well, the banshee has in fact adapted in practical fashion to the mushrooming growth of cities and towns with all their attendant noise. In such places, 'the knock' is often heard instead. The house where a person lies ill receives three clear and loud knocks on the front door, usually late at night. The family knows better than to answer the summons, but is also well aware that there is no turning it back. It is, in fact, a warning of approaching death.

'Oh yes, we have the knock in our family,' said Cliona, a young city nurse, quite matter-of-factly. 'It's because we're MacSweeneys. It's a while now though since we last heard it …'

A senior academic lecturer says the same thing: 'I heard it for my grandmother's death.'

'Myself, I've heard the banshee wail many a time,' says an elderly man on the outskirts of Killarney, 'but my wife there, she has the knock in her family.'

Sightings are far more unusual. After some coaxing, Bríd, a housewife, reveals that her father-in-law, who was in the Army at the time, was driving a truck back from manoeuvres in the early hours of one morning. As they came close to their destination, he saw something strange fluttering in front of an upstairs window of a tall house. At first, he thought it was a sheet left out by accident. But as they drew nearer, he saw a ghostly woman floating there, with blowing robes and long hair. The lorry windows were shut, so they didn't hear her cries, but he drove frantically on to the barracks. His men, who hadn't seen anything, then had to help him down, he was so shaken. The next morning, he discovered that a woman had died in that very house in the early hours of the morning. 'He never forgot that incident for the rest of his life,' said Bríd.

Breda (no relation to Bríd, but also coincidentally named for the goddess Brigit) first heard it when she was a child:

It was late, a dark winter's night, and I was in the back kitchen on my own when I heard this dreadful screaming outside. It was like nothing I'd ever heard in my life before. I ran into the front room and asked my mother if she'd heard, and she said, 'That's the banshee.' I've never forgotten it.

On the next occasion, when she was a teenager, Breda actually saw it – as did several others:

I was in the youth club and this night a bunch of us were coming home. It was just when we were passing a big rock that we saw this white figure floating across in front of the car. I could see it was a woman, in white draperies, with some sort of veil over her head. I got the idea that she was young and kind of elegant, but we only saw it for a moment and it was gone. Myself and two of the lads said, 'What in Heaven's name was that?' and the priest, who must have been as shaken as we were, said, 'I think we'll just say a decade of the Rosary ...'

The banshee doesn't always go to the home of the person who is dying, but can instead cry her warning where that individual rightfully belongs. For example, if someone is near death in, say, Australia or the US, the banshee may be heard crying along the laneways of their former home in Ireland, so that remaining members of the family will take heed.

One time a boy out of the family went to America and he was not long there when he fell seriously ill. One day when the rest of the family were doing their work out in the fields, the bean-sidhe kept crying beside them all day. One night as they were sitting around the fire a shadow passed by the door with a bag in its hand, and that was the very night and the very time the boy died.

One of the worst things to happen to a warrior of ancient times heading to battle would be to come across the Morrigan or banshee by the ford across a river, where she would be washing the blood from his armour and lamenting all the while. This was not, to put it mildly, a very auspicious omen. The Washer at the Ford sends a shiver down every spine when the image occurs in the old legends, and rightly too. Foreseeing your own death would sap the courage of any warrior, however courageous.

What is distinctly eerie, however, is that this ancient practice appears to have travelled with the banshee right down to the present era, as evidenced by writings in the Schools Collection from the 1930s.

It was between twelve and one at night when Micky arrived at the bridge. He looked to his right and was surprised to see a woman washing clothes in one of the pools of the river. Though surprised he was not afraid, because the Autawalla houses were close to the bridge and he expected that the woman who was washing was one from the village, so he shouted to her. 'Why didn't you wait till daylight to wash your clothes mam?' Like a flash the woman and her clothes disappeared …

She was heard opposite Hannons' when Michael died. She was heard another night beside Jim Fallon's. There is a flagstone near the river beside Jim Fallon's house and she was heard washing on the flagstone and crying at the same time. Often long ago the women of the district washed their clothes on that flagstone.

One night Martin King who lived in Clogherboy came to Stephen King in Gurrane-coyle for the loan of a horse and the Bean Sidhe was washing there at the well. She threw a sheet across to him but he did not catch it or it was said if he did that she would pull him in and drown him.

It could be that the banshee in these washing incidents is fulfilling the duties of those who care for the recently passed – laying them out, washing them, putting everything in order. That she is doing it in advance of the death is because her purpose is to warn, to prepare relatives and friends for the loss.

She has been described variously as an ancient hag, a beautiful young girl or a stately woman, always in flowing robes, sometimes white and sometimes black. All, however, agree on her long hair, which she combs continually. (Loosening bound-up hair is one of the classic tokens of mourning.) The comb she uses is variously described as gold or black, but all are agreed that you should never pick it up if you find it by the wayside. If someone is foolish enough so to do, then the banshee will come calling for it that night, tapping at the window and calling constantly. If she does, it must be put in a tongs or on a shovel and held out the window for her to seize. Never let her take it from your hand or you will bear the scars (or lose the hand!). Those who have got close enough to startle or grab at her (obviously thinking she is someone playing a joke) are given a blow across the face, the resultant scars lasting long thereafter.

He was only just lying down on his bed when he heard the weird crying around the house. Someone came and tapped at his window. He got up and looked out through the window and saw the very same little woman which he had seen at the stile. Then he knew that it was the bhean sidhe and that she had come looking for her comb. So he raised the window a small piece and caught the comb with the tongs and put it out through the window to her. She grabbed tongs and comb and pulled them from him. Next day he found the tongs outside the window with the track of five fingers on it.

The classic 1959 film, *Darby O'Gill and the Little People*, includes superb moments featuring the banshee floating and wailing (filmed at the ruined Dunamaise Castle in Co. Laois). The film also has a frightening scene in which the cóiste bodhar, or death coach, appears, journeying down through the night skies, driven by a headless coachman. This visitant does not properly belong to ancient Irish lore, but is likely an import from neighbouring Scotland or further afield. The headless coachman is spoken of in Northern Ireland as the Dullahan, a headless rider dressed all in black, who drives his coach, holding up his own severed head so that it can see all around, and then calling out the name of someone who will die that night. In some legends, the death coach is said to be constructed of human bones, which suggests its origin as considerably further south, perhaps Haiti or some other country where voodoo is practised.

All right, suppose the cóiste bodhar takes a wrong turning and comes down by your house, mistaking the green Irish countryside (or indeed the city street) for Scotland or Haiti. What do you do then? Well, some believe that if you open both the front and the back doors (or indeed the front and back gates) it may well drive past, and hopefully back to where it rightfully belongs.

MALE GODS OF THE OTHERWORLD

One of the most mysterious and certainly the most ancient of the male gods is Crom Cruach, also known as Crom Dubh. Where Danu invited love, he inspired fear, and while the people approached her with celebrations and singing, they came to Crom Cruach as fearful, propitiating supplicants, offering sacrifice to ensure good crops and healthy livestock. His feast day was at the beginning of August, the date now assigned more to Lugh (hence Lughnasa), which marks him, despite his dark visage and reputation, as an early sun god. In a huge stone circle near Lough Gur in Co. Limerick, one gigantic stone stands out, which has always been called Crom Dubh.

Time-honoured festivals still observed today were originally held in his honour. These rituals almost always involve

The Crom Dubh stone at Grange
Stone Circle, showing its huge size.

climbing a high mountain, i.e. getting as close to the sun as possible, to celebrate the god who gives light and warmth, helps the crops to grow and the very people themselves to survive. The festival held at Mount Brandon in Kerry on the last weekend in July every year is still known as Climbing to Crom, although many assume it is honouring St Brendan; and the pilgrimage to Croagh Patrick in Mayo on the same date, though now firmly under the aegis of Christianity, is actually millennia older, and was a pagan ritual observance. Naturally enough, the Church of Rome took care to create documentary evidence that it was here St Patrick challenged the great snake or dragon (i.e. the old religion) and cast it down forever. The lure of climbing to greet the sun, however, has not lessened, and every year the number of pilgrims increases. Reek Sunday, as it has come to be known, is observed in many parts of the country – other names are Garland Sunday or Fraochán Sunday, when the fraocháns, wild Irish bilberries, are ripe.

There was, according to old sources, a special circular mound or fairy fort in Cavan where a gold statue of Crom stood on a hill, surrounded by twelve lesser statues within the fort. Here supplicants would come, bearing gifts and seeking advice or help from those who guarded the sacred place (the druids of the day). A Life of St Patrick (written centuries after his death, by the way) claimed that the saint came here also, and struck Crom and the attendant statues with his crozier, burying them forever from human sight. One wonders why the new religion did not turn them into sacred images (a central Christ and twelve apostles suggests itself), but perhaps they were too awful, too removed from any possibility of Christianisation,

The festival held at Mount Brandon in Kerry on the last weekend in July every year is still known as Climbing to Crom.

to make anything but destruction feasible. Certainly no trace of that golden idol remains today, nor of his twelve disciples. Indeed, the whole area lies empty. One is reminded of that pithy saying, 'History is created by those who write it.'

The Daghda is one of the principal male gods, said to be possessed of great wisdom as well as vast size. One of his most valuable possessions was the Cauldron of Plenty, which furnished the frequent feasts held by the Good People within the lios. This cauldron would obligingly dispense whatever foodstuff or dish a hungry individual desired, changing from one to the next with no difficulty whatsoever. No matter how many guests at the feast, that magic cauldron could never be emptied. In times when hunger was commonplace, and starvation always possible, a place where feasting happened all the time, and a cauldron that was always full, must have been wonders of which to dream.

The Daghda is also possessed of a truly priceless skill – at these feastings within the fairy fort, he plays the Three Magic Tunes on his unique harp. These are the tunes of Sorrow, Joy and War, which inspire all who hear them. They are still said to be heard within fairy forts, and many who overhear them have tried to recapture that haunting music afterwards, but to no avail. That great children's writer, Patricia Lynch, wrote of this tradition in *Brogeen Follows the Magic Tune* (Macmillan, 1952), wherein a quarrelsome tinker gets into a fort by chance, hears and learns the music, and escapes to play it throughout the land. Followed by a leprechaun tasked with removing that memory from the tinker's mind, he instead, surprisingly, proves himself worthy to carry the three magical compositions and thereby to spread good wherever he goes. That, the Good People consider, is enough to warrant his retaining them. Strict in enforcing their rules, certainly, but capable of being fair in appropriate circumstances.

Then there is Goibhniu, the Master Craftsman. While Brigit also watches over crafts, Goibhniu travels the countryside constantly, looking to see that practitioners in every form of craftwork do their very best, and always strive to improve. Smithcraft is his especial care, which is understandable in the context of ancient Ireland and the demands daily survival would have made on its inhabitants. Not only swords and spears for battles with raiders and neighbouring kingdoms, but also ploughshares, wheels, spades – all the tools needed to cultivate the earth. You will still just occasionally hear someone describe himself as 'a humble student of the Master Craftsman'. Incidentally, he is also known as An Gobán Saor, which can be translated as 'free mason'. Such practitioners have been in demand and much honoured since ancient times for their skill in building great structures. We will hear more of that in Chapter VI.

Dian Cécht is son to the Daghda and the god of healing. He is the physician of the Tuatha dé Danann, possessed of incredible skills in curing, even reviving from the dead. In this he reflects many traditional healing skills that were known long ago in Greece and other lands, but were forgotten in later millennia. When battles were to be fought, he would prepare a special well, into which sacred herbs were put. Wounded fighters were plunged into this and were healed of their injuries.

Dian Cécht is most famous for a unique silver arm he made for a king of old, Nuada. In the ancient Second Battle of Moytura, against the savage Fomorians, Nuada had his arm lopped off. Under the old laws, a blemished man could not be king, so Nuada had to give way to another, Breas (the son of a woman of the Tuatha dé Danann and a man of the Fomorians), who proved bad for the country. Dian Cécht, seeing this, set to and created a wondrous, fully flexible, silver arm, which moved as the real one had done, and so Nuada could return to the throne. Whereupon Breas, enraged, returned to his former tribe and incited them to further attacks against his briefly held kingdom. It was ever thus.

Manannán Mac Lir is the god of the sea and all that lives within it. As such, he spends most of his time in his coastal kingdom rather than within the fairy fort, leaving his spouse, the Cailleach Beara, to look after the land. Mermaids, seals, selkies and all forms of fish are under Manannán's care, and he may occasionally be kind to those who venture on the surface of his kingdom, in the frail boats of mankind. An island like Ireland, with its heavily indented coastline, has a great dependence on the sea for its people's livelihood, and thus has need of a god like Manannán to ensure that nets will continue to be filled and voyages completed in safety. But the people must always take care to treat that sea with respect and do nothing to damage its wellbeing – something we would do well to remember today.

Lugh, sometimes called Lugh Lámhfhada or Lugh of the Long Arm, is a proud warrior of the Tuatha dé Danann and a sun god in his own right. It is in his honour that so many festivals are held at Lughnasa, the beginning of August, when the harvest is coming to fruition and the fraocháns or bilberries are ripening. Oddly enough, he is believed to be the grandson of the dreaded Balor of the Evil Eye, the tyrant leader of the Fomorians, whom he finally slays. He is also said to be the father of that hero of so many legends, Cú Chulainn.

Balor of the Evil Eye is certainly not one of the ancient gods of Ireland, but an anti-god, a dreaded figure of legend. He is mentioned here because of his perpetual and pervasive legend, which continues to this day. Fortunately, you are unlikely to meet him at a fairy fort, since such magic places are forever closed against evildoers. Still, it is best to know something about him, in case unlucky chance brings him closer than you would want.

The Fomorians were first and foremost sea pirates, with bases on offshore islands from which to harry and pillage the mainland. Balor – son of Dot, son of Neid, both ruthless pirates before him – is said to have had just one eye in the middle of his forehead, which instantly struck dead any on whom it bent its fearsome gaze. This eye was kept covered under many layers of leather skins until such moments when its power was needed. Then his attendants (who had to lead him, since he was effectively blinded under the eye covering) lifted the layers and the eye could beam out and wreak its dreadful work. Clearly, there are echoes here of both Polyphemus and Medusa of Greek legend, but belief in Balor has continued into living memory. You are most likely to come across this frightening character on the northwest coast of Ireland, particularly around the offshore islands of Sligo.

It is perhaps worth repeating here in brief a point argued in a previous publication (*Stories from the Sea*, O'Brien Press, 2021). Current popular belief holds that Balor had his chief kingdom on Tory Island, several miles off the Donegal coast. Cited as evidence is the ancient name of Balor's main stronghold, Tor Inis. However, when details of the Second Battle of Moytura are studied closely in the oldest records, it is evident that this cannot have been the case. The Tuatha dé Danann, it is recorded, waited until low tide before crossing to the island

Wild waves at Mizen. Is this where Balor died?

and doing battle with the Fomorians. Unfortunately, the tide returned during the height of the fighting, and many of the combatants were drowned on the sands.

That simply couldn't have happened with Tory Island, which is a full 14km (9 miles) off the north coast. But it could, and in all likelihood did, happen at Derinish Island, off Sligo, where today you can still see cattle patiently waiting in line for the low tide to cross from the mainland. (And yes, they do take care to return as they see the tide coming back in! Animals still have strong common sense and keep in touch with nature.)

Cattle still cross to Derinish Island at low tide, just as the Tuatha dé Danaan did to battle with the Fomorians.

The Tory Island legend is very popular, and naturally enough used for touristic purposes, but the ancient records in fact prove Derinish to be the location of Balor's fort. Even the name, Der Inish, is only a slight variation of Tor Inis. And it is worth visiting this stretch of coastline when the tide is changing, just to see, almost like magic, history repeating itself and the old records proved accurate even in today's much-changed world. You don't often get that chance, so seize it.

The Second Battle of Moytura certainly took place in Sligo, and Loch na Súl (rather unimaginatively rendered into English on signposts as Lough Nasool) is said to have been created when Balor's death-dealing eye was driven from his head and fell to the ground here. He was killed by Lugh Lámhfhada or Lugh of the Long Arm, thus fulfilling the prophecy that he would die at the hands of his own grandson. (This odd relationship had come about through a marriage between Balor's daughter and one of the Tuatha dé Danann, arranged as a vain diplomatic attempt at peacemaking.)

There is a second version of his death, though, which says that Balor fled the battlefield, pursued by Lugh, who chased him all the way to Mizen Head, the most southwesterly point in Ireland. There, the younger man finally slew the evil creature and placed his head on a high pinnacle – which immediately shattered into pieces, creating the wild storm-tossed sea cliffs you see today. This is how Mizen Head came by its Irish name – Carn Uí Neid or The Cairn of the Grand-son of Neid, i.e. Balor.

OTHER OTHERWORLD DENIZENS

Another disagreeable creature (or, perhaps more properly, 'thing') that you are fortunately not likely to meet at or around a ráth or lios is the highly unpleasant 'elemental'. This is not so much a ghost or a spirit as a presence, vaguely visible as a greyish shape, but possessed of a hideous odour, and utterly terrifying to anyone unfortunate enough to come across it. Possibly there to protect the interests of the property's ancestors (or perhaps just malevolently present for their own hidden purposes), elementals are generally found in dungeons, cellars or deliberately walled-up rooms in very old buildings. Leap Castle in Co. Offaly is famed as the home of an elemental, but few are courageous enough to search for it. It is not an experience you would want to add to your bucket list.

We have mentioned some of the best-known spirits of the Otherworld who you might find in a fairy fort, but of course these are surrounded by thousands of others. These serve the greater ones, see to the feasting, the music and the dancing, organise the hunts and rides to other forts, and generally enjoy themselves. You are as likely to find them out among the trees, the caves, the cliffs and lakes as well, caring for their individual responsibilities in the natural world.

And on the sea too, which is where the selkies dwell. These Otherworld folk usually appear to our human eyes as seals, with only their great speaking eyes giving a hint of their spirit identities as they swim gracefully past the cliffs or disport themselves in the bay. They will also sunbathe on rocks that rise above the water at low tide, but to see them as they really

Selkies can come out at night and shed their disguises on the rocks.

are, you need to go out at midnight, with the tide at its lowest reach. That is when the selkies come ashore, shed their disguising fur skins, and dance on the sands in their real, beautiful forms. You will need to keep well under cover though, as the slightest hint of a watcher will send them flying to grasp their fur skins and disappear again under the sea.

Many are the stories told of young men who fall in love with beautiful selkie maidens, and manage to seize their fur coats. If you do this, apparently, she is forced to come home with you and even marry you and bear your children. If she should discover where you have hidden her lost coat, however, she will return to the sea, leaving you and her children grieving. There are several families on the west coast of Ireland who claim to have descended from selkie matings with humans. And maybe they have, who knows?

Even if you don't manage to catch a glimpse of them dancing on the shoreline at midnight, there is still a magical experience to be found fairly easily, and that is the enchanting 'singing of the selkies'. Find a remote cliff where the rocks far below offer good resting places for these beautiful sea creatures, then sit and wait. Sooner or later, you will hear their haunting voices drifting up to you, singing in a strange language of their homes far beneath the waves, of their lives and the things they see on their wanderings. It's difficult to leave such a place and such an experience.

Now, quite different to all of these is the leprechaun. This individual really is an enigma, being a solitary worker, a little man, much in contrast to the tall, noble Good People (the Irish luchorpán means, literally, small body). He is outside their general gathering, yet still inextricably part of it. Stories involving him go right back to the oldest records, the most famous being that of Iubdhan and the Porridge Pot. Engagingly, this tale stems from a legend found scribbled on a scrap of vellum amid a bundle of legal papers from the eighth century. Clearly the scribe got bored and decided to write down the amusing story as it had been told to him by some learned person.

Iubhdan, we are told, was king of the Tiny People, but of course neither he nor his country had any idea of their being lesser folk. Indeed, he would brag frequently at banquets about his greatness, and how nobody could match either himself or his kingdom in splendour. And his subjects would obediently cheer and agree.

One day, however, the court poet told him that there was indeed a land with far larger people in it, the Kingdom of

Giants in Ulster, far over the sea, ruled by King Fergus. Disbelieving, Iubhdan and his queen (Bebo by name) set off for this mythical land with the intention of proving the poet utterly wrong. Arriving at dawn, while everyone was still asleep, they set out to explore, and were fascinated to discover a gigantic pot of porridge, steaming gently in an enormous kitchen.

Iubhdan decided he wanted to taste this porridge before the giants awoke, but while trying to sample a spoonful, both he and Bebo fell into the pot. When the servants of Fergus found the tiny couple struggling in the porridge, they were delighted and brought the pair forthwith to King Fergus. He, equally delighted, gave them every comfort and luxury and kept them at his court for entertainment, refusing to let them go back to their own land. After a year, however, Iubhdan exchanged his most valuable possession for their freedom – a pair of magical shoes that would allow the wearer to walk not only on water, but underneath it too. They then returned to the Kingdom of the Tiny People, having learned, presumably, that not all people are the same and it is as well to realise that you are not necessarily the biggest or most important.

It seems that, having heard the story of his travels, some of Iubhdan's followers decided to come and live in this wondrous land of Ireland, since they have been here ever since. (Incidentally, the gift kicked back, as Otherworld gifts are wont to do, since Fergus used the shoes to fight a dreadful lake monster who in the end brought him to his death. You never can be sure what you are getting from a leprechaun.)

The tale might well have given Jonathan Swift the inspiration for his classic *Gulliver's Travels*, in which the eponymous hero visits both the land of tiny people and the land of giants. And that pair of magical shoes could be a clue to the very strong tradition that the leprechaun makes all the shoes for the Good People, sitting in a corner of the fairy fort endlessly tapping, cutting and stitching. Riding boots of softest green suede; buckled black dancing shoes; shining silver slippers for feasting; he is adept at making them all. It is said that if you can ever persuade a leprechaun to make you a pair of shoes, you will dance your way right out of your house and never stop until you reach the door of a fairy fort – which will fly open magically to let you in. Your eventual return, shoeless or otherwise, is not to be depended on though, so perhaps it is wiser to stay with your everyday shoe shop.

A man named Larkin was taking a stroll one nice summer's evening convenient to the ring of this fort just after sunset. He thought he heard a sharp tapping not much larger than the tick of a large clock and on looking around he was surprised to see a small elf not more than eight inches in height sitting under bracken and he was cobbling a very tiny boot. Larkin stole round a whin and made a grab for the cobbler who slipped through his fingers and got away, but with the sudden fright he left the boot behind him. Larkin picked up the boot, which was no larger than a thimble. He went on his way looking at it. In a little while he heard a voice saying, 'Fág an bhróg in do dhiaidh.' [Leave the boot behind you.] He went on, not listening, again he heard a number of voices saying, 'Fág an bhróg in do dhiaidh.' Larkin dropped the boot and all went well again.

On fine days, leprechauns seize the opportunity to go outside for a while, and are often heard tapping away at their work with a little gold hammer underneath a sunny gorse bush or hawthorn tree. The popping noise made by gorse seeds cracking open in hot weather is very similar to the sound made by his hammer. He himself is very rarely seen, though, and if you do happen to catch sight of him, it is best to be ready to grab his coat before he sees you. Once you have him, keep a tight hold until he tells you where his pot of gold is hidden. That treasure is one of the facts most firmly believed about the leprechaun. He guards a treasure, usually concealed at the end of the rainbow, but often close by where he is currently working. And indeed, in any landscape where treasure may have been concealed in times of war long, long ago, it is entirely feasible that he should be its guardian.

A story from Co. Cavan demonstrates that you have to be very clever indeed to beat the wit of a leprechaun. A man who had been visiting friends was coming home late at night by one of the fairy ráths. When he came near the fort, he heard the noise of a hammer. He knew the stories of leprechauns hiding crocks of gold, so he went up to the fort and looked in. There was a little man mending boots. The man asked him civilly to find a crock of gold for him. 'I will indeed,' said the leprechaun, 'if you lift up that stone there at your foot.' So he stooped and lifted it up, and when he looked again, he saw that the fairy had disappeared.

Another example is that classic of the farmer managing to seize a leprechaun in one of his fields, and refusing to let him go until he showed the exact location of the gold. 'Under that very ragwort [buachalán buidhe],' said the little man, pointing to a lone plant, standing tall and golden. Quickly, the man pulled off his bright green sock and tied it round the plant. Then, letting the leprechaun go (and that fellow scuttled off pretty quickly, as you can imagine), the farmer ran home to fetch a spade. Back he came in double-quick time, only to stop, appalled. The field was now full of tall golden ragworts, every single one of them sporting a bright green sock! It would appear that the leprechaun does possess (and does not scruple to use) a reasonable amount of those magical powers enjoyed by the other Good People.

Some say he is related to the English brownie, and only over here on a visit, but that is a slanderous suggestion. He is as Irish as the rest of the Gentry and has been part of our legends since time began. Although he is far smaller than those tall, pale figures and keeps himself to himself as a rule, he belongs within the fairy fort too.

Although he could not exactly be described as one of our spirit ancestors, the púca is also very much an Irish Otherworld figure. Strongly believed in, the púca appears in countless legends and features in many real-life experiences. Also variously spelled pouka, pooka or phouca, this strange and mischievous creature roams the countryside looking for ways to throw human beings off balance and interfere with their lives. As far as records show, he isn't dangerous, but does love to put a little unexpected excitement into the life of unwary travellers on their journeys. He is emphatically a creature of the wild open spaces, never caring to venture into urban environments. So you should be safe enough in a city. Although you never know.

Places around Ireland that are named for the púca are legion. Poula Phouka, a waterfall in the Wicklow mountains; The Poulaphuca mountains in Clare; Carrigaphooka outside Macroom; Lios na bPuca in Kerry (firmly translated into English as Beaufort, refusing any hint of the Otherworld); and many more.

Healing wells were often called púca pools before Christianity firmly gave them new saintly names. Puck Fair, held at Killorglin in August since time immemorial, displays a fine horned goat as part of the fair's tradition, and there is more than a nod to the ancient púca spirit there.

Most often, the púca appears in the guise of a horse, usually black, but that doesn't mean you should ignore ponies,

That innocent, small pony rolling an eye at you could well be the púca in disguise.

The púca can also appear in the shape of a wild goat.

donkeys, mules or especially goats. This is a spirit who likes to shape-change, and could well be that innocent, small pony rolling an eye at you over the fence, or that wild, horned goat you come across on the mountainside, peacefully chewing the cud.

His usual trick is to come up unexpectedly behind you at night, throw you on his back and gallop across the country-side, over hills and through bogs, until, towards morning, he dumps you in a wet marsh or a clump of brambles. Then you have a long way to walk home, and some explaining to do about the hour and the state of your clothes. Unbelievers may suggest that such happenstance could have more to do with over-indulgence at the pub rather than a fairy spirit, but it is worth remembering to take care and never accept what seems a tempting offer of a lift home from an unknown horse.

There are several interesting legends, including one from Co. Cork, where a stream was known as Glaisín a' Phúca (the little stream of the púca). Locals would not normally pass it at night, but it chanced that one man had to hurry on horseback for the doctor late one evening, as his brother was very sick.

When he came to Glaisín a' Phúca, a little distance east of the new bridge, the horse stopped and would go no farther. Just then a man came out of Glaisín a' Phúca and led the horse into town. The man went to the doctor's house and told the doctor to go to his brother. He then came out and got on his horse again, but the same man came again and led the horse through the town and past Glaisín a' Phúca. He then spoke for the first time, and told the man on horseback not to ever again pass Glaisín a' Phúca at that hour of the night.

Another story seems to suggest that the púca frequents the shoreline and the sea as well as the land. Some fishermen regularly went mackerel fishing at night, and frequently saw a black horse actually emerge from the water and gallop up the beach. It happened that one fisherman left some of his catch down on the shore and sent his two sons down to fetch it later that night. They were chased under a tarpaulin by the púca and hid there, trembling in fear, until the welcome light of day.

It is said that if you are courageous and stand up to the púca, you will get home safely, but it can't always be relied on. Stories are numerous of men who, after one encounter, wore spurs at night thereafter when walking home. If snatched by the spirit animal, they would use these vigorously until he threw them off – hopefully not too far from their dwelling. One such case, with an intriguing twist, occurred in Co. Limerick, where the spurred rider was indeed thrown safely off, but the following night was actually approached by the púca, who asked him, in Irish, if he still had 'those sharp things' on him. They had a brief discussion, apparently parted friends, and the farmer was never troubled by the mischievous animal again. There are other instances of the púca only speaking in the native tongue, which is interesting, demonstrating that he belongs to an older time, before colonists endeavoured to stamp out our own language.

There is at least one story, however, showing that it is not wise to mistreat this spirit creature. At a place known as the Pooka's Pool in the midlands, where passers-by were often taken for joyrides by Himself, a heedless youth claimed that he could beat the animal any time, and teach him better manners. When he dug vicious spurs into his mount, however, he was thrown off into the pool, where he drowned. The local people were unanimous in saying that he should not have tried to injure one of Them, as otherwise he would have been unharmed.

This solitary spirit (he does not congregate with others of Themselves, preferring to work alone in his beloved wild countryside) is much associated with Samhain or Hallow-E'en. There is a tradition that says he gallops over blackberry bushes at this time, and it is therefore inadvisable to gather them after that date. This is particularly interesting, as in the north of England and Scotland they say that blackberries must not be picked after Michaelmas, at the end of September, 'because the devil throws his cloak over them then'. There is a definite indication here of the gentler climate of Ireland, where the first frost comes later, and fruit is palatable for at least a month longer.

So what to do if you are suddenly accosted by a fiery black horse or a wild, horned goat late at night and taken for an unexpected gallop across the hills? Best to hold on (although you won't fall off until he intends you to) and enjoy the experience. Just hope that he doesn't drop you too far from your intended road home.

Of course, any animal you meet on the road may be one of Themselves in disguise. A hare, for instance, is a favoured disguise, not least because of its fleetness in escaping capture. Wise women are reputed to take on this guise while out seeking to wreak mischief, but it could also just as easily be one of the Good People shape-changing while travelling, so as not to attract attention.

The Irish hare – or is it one of Themselves in disguise?

There are strange stories attached to gatherings of hares. An elderly vet in Kerry recounted a story of one Midsummer morning when he was slowly driving home after being out all night. On a hill overlooking a fairy fort, he stopped to watch the sun rise, and only then saw the hares gathered around the mound. They were all sitting up tall, stock still, apparently watching the dawn just as he was. 'I didn't move, but the hairs rose on the back of my neck. It was like nothing else I'd ever seen.'

We can confirm a similar experience ourselves, when we were out very early one morning in West Cork, trying to get a shot of the sun rising behind a particular ráth. As we parked on the road above the mound, we noticed several hares running towards it

The Morrigan can take the form of a harshly croaking raven.

from different directions. Of course, we stayed still and silent, watching incredulously as more and more hares came down to that circle. One even came across a hill above us and hurried across the road, not even glancing at our car, in his haste to join the gathering. We stayed until the sun was up and the hares were slowly dispersing. Driving home, we couldn't quite believe what we had witnessed.

The madness of March, do I hear you say comfortably? Well, a bit late for that in both cases, although it certainly could have had something to do with mating rituals. But specifically at fairy forts?

A raven, as indicated earlier, should always be greeted civilly with a 'good morning' and a bow, or at least a polite nod of the head. This tradition appears to have been transferred to magpies in recent years, but they are relative newcomers to Ireland, whereas the raven, as we know, could be the banshee or Morrigan in disguise. The wren, acknowledged as the king of birds, passes between our world and Theirs with ease, and was frequently used by the druids of old to foretell the future. (Not, we hasten to add, by killing it, but by sharply observing its behaviour as it flitted from one perch to another. Today we analyse and test scientifically, but back then they watched, listened and learned.)

Cattle have always been vitally important in Ireland, and if you were fortunate, your herd might be augmented by the unexpected appearance of a small white cow with red ears. This, you could be sure, was a fairy cow, which usually emerged from a nearby lake and took up her place peacefully in the field. If you treated such a visitor well and respectfully, she

The wren, king of all birds, passes between this and the Otherworld
with ease.

would give you generous milk and also calves; but treat her badly and she would simply say goodbye and stroll back to her own home in the Otherworld.

Cats, of course, cross between both worlds all the time, and know far more than they will tell. Whereas a dog will follow his owner and do as he is told, you can never get a cat to do other than it already intends to. They follow their own path, which often leads through the veil to the Other Side. That's why they so often go out at night, to meet with Themselves and share their knowledge. It is claimed that if you tell the family cat something important, it will shortly afterwards leave the house and hurry off to inform the Good People. Watch and see if it doesn't do just that.

There are many instances of cats being seen in and around fairy forts, and one of the spirit animals said to dwell in our caves is the cat sidhe or fairy cat, a huge, black feline with gleaming green eyes. He isn't renowned for charm or good manners, though, so if you come across him, beware of those sharp claws.

The main thing to remember is that almost any creature you see along the road could well be one of Themselves in disguise. It is good practice to salute all, avoid injuring or insulting, and maintain peaceful co-existence as much as possible. They were here a long time before us, and will continue to care for this land long after we are gone.

Uragh Stone Circle has an incredible setting.

CHAPTER VI

HOW CAME THESE GREAT STONES?

The fairy forts, ráths and lios are widely believed to be entrances to the Otherworld, but the Good People are to be found in many other places too, since they travel widely to see that every corner of Ireland is looked after and cared for. Ancient megaliths, hills and caves; lakes, rivers, wells and islands; wherever there is a separation, a division between the world we know and the one that is veiled from our eyes; in all such places there may be secret entrances and the Gentry may be present.

Solitary trees too (especially hawthorn), as well as forests, are often inhabited by spirits, and certain hidden routes, invisible to our eyes but clearly defined to Their eyes, are fairy paths and should never be blocked. All around us in the landscape are hints and clues to the presence of our ancient nature spirits who are still guarding its wellbeing. In this and the following chapter, some of those other links to the Otherworld will be looked at.

The island of Ireland is incredibly rich in ancient stone structures, megaliths that seem to defy reality in their sheer size and complexity, their wealth of the oldest carvings and artefacts. Little wonder then that the Celts, on arriving here, took it for granted that they must be the work of the gods themselves – surely no mere humans could have created such works. Enormous built complexes incorporating numerous passages and chambers; tall dolmens with dizzyingly huge capstones; mysterious stone circles and rows. They might seem to our modern eyes more like film sets, built with polystyrene and paint rather than the intractable weight of stone. But massive stone works they are, and standing here for millennia. How on earth was it done?

Carved stones at the entrance to Newgrange.

Indeed, that is the big question: how was it achieved, back in the mists of time, without any of the technology and engineering machinery we enjoy (or endure) today? Built long before the Celts came from Spain, the Christians from Rome, the much later colonists from nearby Britain. Most, if not all, are older than Stonehenge, older even than the Pyramids. Newgrange in Co. Meath, for example, predates the Great Pyramids by at least 3,000 years, and Stonehenge by 1,000 years. One of the cairns at Carrowkeel – a magnificent, spread-out megalithic complex in Sligo on the western coast, though far smaller than Newgrange – is estimated to predate that mighty structure by yet another 700 years. Who envisaged them, caused them to be constructed? For what purpose? And, most of all: how? It seems impossible, and yet they are here, striking features of the past still standing in our modern landscape.

Most importantly, all of these magnificent monuments were built in the traditional circular shape that also characterises the lios or fairy fort. As we have seen in the opening chapter, the observance and acknowledgement of the eternal circle is central to the ancient practices and beliefs of Ireland. Later civilisations across the world would create vast structures with hard edges, sharpening corners and straightening lines to build square or oblong monuments, but in this land, the vital importance and power of the circle and its link to the very wheel of life was never forgotten.

PASSAGES, PORTALS, COURTS AND WEDGES

It might be a good idea at this juncture to emphasise that although many of the best-known megalithic structures are

Kilclooney dolmen in Donegal with its tiny fellow dolmen close by.

identified in archaeological circles as 'tombs' of one kind or another – passage, portal, court, wedge, etc. – there is no real evidence for this, or even notional agreement as to what their original purposes may have been. The largest complexes of all, at Brú na Bóinne (which includes Newgrange), are classified as passage tombs. Court tombs are so named for a flat area laid out in front of the entrance, and portal tombs for their visually impressive entrances. Wedge tombs are smaller, often just two or three stones leaning together. Again, as with fairy forts, the fabric of such structures are often dictated by the building materials available locally.

But 'tombs'? Uncertain, to the extent of 'unlikely'. Sometimes human bones have been excavated, more often not. That they are designed to have a highly visible entrance, often oriented to face the sunrise or sunset, is provable, but beyond that, we still don't know what went on in these structures.

From a practical point of view, it really is unlikely that a complex the size of Newgrange, taking many years to create, involving many thousands of workers and incredible amounts of enormous stones, would be built as the burial chamber of one individual, however great in his or her time. That they were ritual centres, at which many people assembled at special times, is far more likely, with the occasional ceremonial interment of the bones of a noted leader taking place.

Their construction, whenever and however it happened, does in fact foreshadow the much later building of vast cathedrals and abbeys across Europe in a newer style of angles and sharp corners, where the chosen few might also be honoured by final burial within their sacred crypts or grounds. Those later buildings, many still standing and admired today, were made possible by the driving power of Christianity. What drove the ancient ones of Ireland? The earliest settlers are often described as 'simple hunter-gatherers'. To put it mildly, that doesn't exactly match with the achievements we can still see in our prehistoric stone monuments, their curves constantly echoing belief in the power of the circle.

The question of why these surviving structures were built in the first place is something about which historians and archaeologists are never tired of theorising. Commemorations and burial places of powerful leaders? Ritual sites to honour their own gods? Focal points for the gathering of great hosts? Even power centres for communicating with worlds and planets beyond? We just don't know. We can guess, we can have our own favourite theories, but we cannot know for certain.

Another important point too, not always thought about by the visitor: Why were they built in those specific places? The undeniable fact that they still convey a strong sense of mystery and hidden power is held to have a great deal to do with their exact locations, on sites chosen with the knowledge and skill of the ancients.

It is believed that the sites for these buildings were specially chosen to harness and focus the natural powers of the Earth, its lines of energy. The late Michael Poynder (*Pi in the Sky: A revelation of the ancient Celtic wisdom tradition*) spent three decades dowsing sites in Ireland and mapping their earth stars. He believed Brú na Bóinne to be part of a massive network of lines that pass through many important ancient sites.

The powerful energy and presence at Newgrange has been said by many to be particularly evident at the time of the full moon, the solstices and the equinoxes. Underground water systems seem to have a great deal to do with this, although we do not yet know enough to say precisely why, but dowsing is still a popular practice at many ancient megaliths. Our ancestors, of course, would have been expert dowsers. After all, even today, huge and successful well-digging companies still rely on a practised dowser to find the right place to drill. All that expensive equipment, and yet the little old man with the forked stick (or bent wire coathanger) still climbs out of the truck and sets off across the site to locate water sources deep below ground. Only then can the big boys get going. (What damage they are doing to the ancient lines of power is another matter entirely.)

And how long did such amazing feats of construction take? Years, most certainly. Did the labourers willingly give up so much of their time? And if so, why, when they could have been dealing with the more urgent task of hunting for food and ensuring their own personal survival? Either the leaders of such people must have been powerful indeed, or the entire population believed intensely in the importance of what they were doing and welcomed the chance to be a part of it.

Back in ancient Ireland, there must have been a powerful incentive and an unshakeable belief. As Eugene O'Curry, the renowned professor of Irish history and archaeology, once said when viewing this incredible heritage of stone, 'What marvellous manuscripts, if only we could read them.'

When you consider the overall vast size of these monuments, the weight of the individual stones and the huge effort needed to move them, along with the incredible design and specific placement of these structures, it is not surprising to find strong belief that not only were they built by our ancient gods, but that such spirits might still be found here. Indeed, many of today's visitors become gradually aware of a strong but invisible presence when exploring such legendary places. It is understandable then that incomers like the Celts assumed that their dark entrance portals led to the Otherworld. From that, it was an easy step to believe the same of the oldest earthen and stone enclosures with their dark entrances to souterrains, and thus finally of all ringforts, ráths, dúns and lios.

How these greatest of Irish monuments were planned and designed, how the huge, intractable and supremely heavy

masses of stone were sourced and actually brought to the chosen sites, and how they were moved into their permanent positions, is something we shall probably never know. Supplies for Newgrange, for instance, certainly came from Co. Down, some 100km to the north, and from Wicklow, about the same distance to the south. To give just one example, the capstone on magnificent Brownshill Dolmen, a portal tomb in Co. Carlow, at an estimated 150 tonnes, is thought to be the heaviest in Europe. Just to stand before it, rearing up arrogantly on its green grassy circle, surrounded by blowing cornfields, is to feel your breath taken away. Do we need reminding yet again that these were constructed unknown thousands of years before man invented mechanical lifters and diggers?

Clearly, those who built them must not only have established exactly the most propitious place to place these gigantic megaliths, but also knew precisely what they wanted and how they should be designed (and where, we might ask, did they gain that information?). They knew where to find the craftsmen, who in their turn knew where to source the specific materials needed, and how to instruct the workers in their truly Herculean task.

They must have had excellent knowledge of geology and geometry as well as physics, especially the principles of leverage (you would certainly need some knowledge of that last skill when dealing with those gigantic stones). And, above all, geomancy (literally, 'earth divination') – those methods that note and interpret geographical features; the patterns formed by soil, rocks or sand; the presence of water underneath. Apparently the strong energy created by the presence of crystal quartzite, to take just one example, can be felt by anyone who knows what to look for. Clearly, all that information was available in an ancient network that extended who knows how far around the world.

Yes, before the internet, before WhatsApp, before email, such knowledge was obviously there for those who knew how to access it. Perhaps the 'global village', regarded as a modern concept, has been around longer than we thought? It is no accident that one of the greatest of the ancient Irish gods was Goibniú, the Master Craftsman, also known in legend as the Gobán Saor or Freemason. Throughout the ages, the most skilled free masons were always honoured and valued, much in demand wherever a great new building was to be constructed. Was there a network of such eminent craftsmen travelling throughout ancient Europe? It looks like there was. And did the Master himself lend a hand? Quite possibly.

Without doubt, Brú na Bóinne (the Palace of the Boyne), which encompasses Newgrange, Knowth and Dowth in the Boyne Valley, is the foremost of our ancient megalithic treasures. The scale of these great structures, indeed the complexity and number of individual sites, beggars belief, as does their surviving richness of stone carvings. Newgrange was first excavated in a rather haphazard manner in the late seventeenth century, and recognised as the Brú na Bóinne of legend, a place of ancient power and a known residence of the Good People. It was thus on the very early tourist trail, with inevitable damage caused by treasure-seekers and collectors. However, it was only as recently as the 1960s that the distinguished archaeologist Professor MJ O'Kelly began his careful and painstaking professional excavation. Newgrange's greatest secret (should we add 'so far'?) was then discovered:

'It was around the middle of December and pretty cold,' he told our enthralled class of archaeology students at Cork University several years later. 'We had more or less cleared the passage through into the central chamber – it had been a matter of crawling on all fours up to then. I was standing there on my own, looking around me, and rubbing the dirt off my hands, when this thin ray of light came over my shoulder through a hidden aperture, and touched the earthen floor. It was like the hand of God!'

You never forget hearing something like that from the man who discovered it.

It was first established on that December day that at the winter solstice, the rising sun strikes the face of the passage tomb in one specific place, where a tiny aperture and tunnel had been specially created. The first rays thus pierce the entire thickness of the wall, move along the narrow earthen passage within and illuminate the central chamber.

It is fascinating to consider just how the builders of New-grange might have planned and executed that specific feature, on which the power and importance of the whole layout depended. Did they already know the exact point at which the rays of the rising sun would strike a particular point? Or did they wait patiently until the shortest day in the year, to mark it on that exact spot? It is probable that they had already marked the circle of the year by sundials and the shadows thrown by tall standing stones. But did they take into account microscopic shifts and changes in the Earth's orbit? We know that gravitational pull from Jupiter and Saturn changes our orbit slightly from time to time – did the ancients know that too? Yes, again, very probably. And allowed for it too. It has to be emphasised yet again how much they knew that we, with all our scientific advancements, have lost.

Today this seeming miracle of solar power still happens, just as it did so many centuries ago, and crowds from all over the world swarm to be there for the experience. Needless to say, very, very few can gain entrance to the chamber itself, and applicants queue up years ahead, but still thousands come to stand outside and wait for the great moment when the sun rises, signalling the drawing out of the days, the retreat of the dark hours. (Note: If you do get there and stand shivering outside in the pre-dawn chill, don't feel cheated if the sun rises but is entirely hidden by clouds. It happens fairly often. This is Ireland in December after all. And the Good People like to have their little joke from time to time. Just take in the whole experience and be thankful.)

You might have better luck trying for Dowth at the winter solstice, as it is now known that the orientation of the two great megaliths allows the sunset to illuminate the chamber at Dowth and rise the next morning to illuminate New-grange. It is the true experience of death and rebirth within the never-ending circle of the year. Apart from that one day in midwinter when they open the gates, however, Dowth is still under excavation and not generally open to the public as yet. Better check beforehand that it will be open when you go, rather than just turning up in hope.

Naturally enough, there are many legends and stories of the Otherworld and the Good People linked to Brú na Bóinne, and it is fitting that the most famous one involves the rising and setting of the sun at the solstice as well as the eternal theme of love. Elcmar, husband of Boann, goddess of the River Boyne, was the first owner of this great palace fort. The Daghda, chief male god of the Otherworld, whom we met in Chapter V, fell madly in love with Boann and desired her for his own. Clearly this was going to be difficult with Elcmar around, so he arranged to have the husband sent off on a day's journey. While Elcmar is absent, the Daghda achieves the assignation with Boann and gets her with child. To make sure their tryst is never discovered, the all-powerful god makes the sun stand still for a full nine months, so that beyond the palace only a day has passed. The son of Boann and the Daghda is therefore born on the same day that he is conceived – at the winter solstice – and Elcmar never suspects that the child is not his own. Or perhaps he does, but is wise enough not to raise questions that might anger a god.

The child is Aengus Óg, god of love in the ancient pantheon. He is always linked to birds, especially the swans that can often be seen floating gracefully on the River Boyne. He and his true father, the Daghda, take over the palace on the Boyne and live there in harmony for some time. Until, that is, Aengus decides he would like it for himself. He tricks his father into letting him take it by asking the Daghda to give it to him for a day and a night. His father consents, whereupon Aengus Óg points out that eternity consists of day and night, and so he has been given Brú na Bóinne permanently. One would expect his father to refuse or at least remonstrate, but apparently parental love conquers all, and so the great palace becomes the home of the God of Love thereafter.

There are other, later legends linked to Newgrange, also treating of birth rather than death, i.e. the rising of the sun rather than its setting. The great Celtic hero Cúchulainn is said to have been born here – he too came of a human–divine mating, his mother being Deichtine, sister of King Conchobar mac Nessa, and his father the sun god Lugh. Again, the sun and its vital importance is at the centre of the legend.

This theme – a god descending to create a miraculous child (always a son, one notes) with a mortal woman – is repeated throughout ancient annals all over the world. The Greek Zeus and the Roman Jupiter were both renowned for this energetic practice. It was an idea that the later Christian Church was to seize on and incorporate into its own teachings with great success.

It is only fair to mention a slight downside to the fame of Brú na Bóinne. It is one of the must-visit places on every tourist's list, as well as that of schools and special interest groups, and so it is crowded to capacity almost all year round. Booking in advance is essential, and you will need patience when faced with the queues, the difficulty of parking and all the hassle of a very popular attraction with worldwide fame. Allowing for all that, it's somewhere you ought to go, at least once.

But if you want to experience the same heightened sense of wonder, delight and amazement that Professor O'Kelly felt back in the 1960s, maybe you would be better off searching through old maps, getting out into the countryside and finding your own, as yet undiscovered ancient site that the Otherworld has been guarding. Well, probably not entirely undiscovered, as most of Ireland's prehistoric monuments have by now been identified and mapped. However, only a few have been developed into visitor sites, so it is still very possible to stand by one that is thousands of years old and experience something special for you alone, perhaps hear a whisper from Themselves.

Carrowkeel, in Co. Sligo on the west coast, is pretty remote and less adjusted for tourism than Newgrange, but splendid in its spread of megalithic structures, covering a huge area. You could walk here for days, seeing something new at every step. Similarly at Carrowmore, overseen at a distance by the great mountain of Knocknarea, surmounted by the cairn that is said to be the burial place of the legendary Queen Maeve.

The wind has bundled up the clouds high over Knocknarea
And thrown the thunder on the stones for all that Maeve can
say …
(WB Yeats, 'Red Hanrahan's Song About Ireland')

Mushera Mountain in Co. Cork, not far from Millstreet, is not particularly well known, and is passed by without a second glance by most travellers on their way to Killarney. However, it has a long reputation in the neighbourhood as a seriously 'airy' place. This does not mean fresh and blowy – although that's certainly true – but refers rather to Otherworld or fairy influences that are believed to permeate its slopes and to touch all who travel there. Drive its steep, winding roads and you will see all kinds of ancient structures, from wedge tombs and dolmens to ringforts and stone circles, scattered over its slopes. Clearly Mushera (more properly Mushera Mór, or Big Mushera; Mushera Beg, or Little Mushera, nestles to its west) was an important focal point and ceremonial gathering place many thousands of years ago.

The two hills can sometimes be seen clearly, but sometimes they are shrouded in mist, indicating either that the Good People are staying home, or that they are planning to set out on their travels again. And it has its own legends, including even sightings of Themselves, notably the banshee. As mentioned in Chapter V, a group of young people returning from a dance in Millstreet in the 1970s were shocked to see a wraith-like white figure floating in front of the car just at the foot of Mushera. The woman who remembered the incident said they had no doubt at all it was the banshee they had seen.

Another story concerns a family of several generations that came out to walk on the mountain not many years ago. The grandfather was feeling unwell, so they left him sitting in the car at the foot of the hill and went on up the narrow road. Some way up, they met a woman dressed all in black coming down. She looked keenly at them as she passed, and said, 'He's all right now, he's fine.' Then she passed on. They looked back, startled – and she was nowhere to be seen. A little concerned, they turned and went down again, only to find the grandfather lying quietly dead in the car. There was no sign of the woman in black. Was it Herself coming to give them reassurance that he was at peace? You can never tell what will happen on Mushera.

Poulnabrone, in the amazing stone landscape that is the Burren.

Dolmens – skeletons in the landscape

Also known as tables of the ancient heroes, as cromlechs, or as giants' graves, these stark megalithic structures are familiar from images in any Irish tourist literature. Poulnabrone, in the middle of the vast stone wonderland that is the Burren in Co. Clare, has appeared on websites all over the world. Striking it certainly is, standing alone on an endless limestone pavement that stretches to the horizon, while the winds blow round it ceaselessly, as they have always done. But there are many other dolmens too, whatever part of the country you are in, and all of a size to make you gasp as you wonder, not only how on earth they were constructed, but also how they have survived so long. They were solidly built in the first place, evidently!

Structurally, dolmens are further examples of the so-called 'tombs' already mentioned, consisting of a large roofing slab supported by two or three upright monoliths. What were once great portals or doorways in vast circular or oval mounds are now open to the four winds, but the very sparsity of their sharp outlines lends them extra drama in the landscape. Their strength and power are really something to discover and experience for yourself.

Kilclooney dolmen, between Ardara and Portnoo close to the Donegal coast, is spectacular, with an enormous capstone over four metres long by 3.7 metres wide at its front. Staggeringly, it is nearly a metre thick in places. The whole structure was probably once much larger, and what we see today is perhaps merely the entranceway to a mound of far greater size. What is intriguing is another tiny dolmen standing nearby with its capstone fallen. You can't help wondering for what purpose it was built.

The tradition is that if you can toss three pebbles onto the capstone of Kilclooney dolmen, making a wish at the same time, your wish will come true. The same belief attaches to several other dolmens, such as Proleek on the Cooley Peninsula in Co. Louth and Leac an Scail in Co. Kilkenny (said to be Ireland's tallest dolmen at five metres in elevation) – in fact anywhere the surviving height of the structure makes such a challenge reasonably difficult. Have a go – although always be aware that the Gentry may have their own entertaining ways of granting your wish, which might not quite be what you had in mind!

Goward dolmen in Co. Down is another breathtaking sight, with its gigantic capstone (estimated to weigh fifty tonnes) now slightly slipped from its portal supports. Standing by a quiet lane, it is known very casually among locals

Aughnacliffe dolmen in Longford looks precariously balanced.

The Labby Rock in Sligo, a strange megalithic structure indeed.

as 'Pat Kearney's big stone', after the man who lived in a thatched cottage right next to it for many years. And there are so many more. The Labby Rock and the Giant's Griddle in Co. Sligo. Aughnacliff, by Lough Gowna in Co. Longford, surely one of the strangest-looking still to be seen, apparently teetering precariously on its support stones. Little (well, relatively speaking) Gaulstown dolmen, near Kilmeaden in Co. Waterford, sitting serenely in a clearing amid thick woodland, looking very much at home. Which it is of course – it has been there forever, while we are just passing through.

What is seen in a dolmen today, however dramatic and photogenic, is really no more than the skeleton of the original structure. This basic framework, like those of other so-called 'tomb' monuments, would have been covered with earth and stones, gradually acquiring a thick layer of grass and turf, turning them

into their true form as fairy mounds. Small wonder then that stories abound of strange things seen, strange sounds heard, around these magnificent relics of a mysterious past.

There are many semi-collapsed dolmens, and also great standing stones that have wearied of being upright for millennia and have assumed a more relaxed, recumbent position on the ground. A lot of these have been given the name Diarmuid and Gráinne's Bed, after the legendary love story from the Fianna Cycle of legends.

Briefly, this was the way it happened: Fionn Mac Cumhaill (or Finn McCool), great leader and hero, is widowed, and his advisers select Gráinne, the beautiful daughter of King Cormac Mac Airt, as a suitable new bride. At the betrothal feast, however, Gráinne is dismayed to discover that her future husband is old and worn, and her eye alights on one of Fionn's young warriors, the handsome Diarmuid. She challenges him to run away with her before the marriage. He at first refuses, out of loyalty to his leader, but capitulates when she places a geis or obligation on him so to do. (The geis is an ancient Irish custom, obliging the recipient to obey its dictates or risk dishonour or even death.)

Pursued by the furious and frustrated Fionn, the young couple flee across the length and breadth of Ireland, never daring to sleep two nights in the same place. Intriguingly, again out of loyalty, Diarmuid holds out as long as possible against Gráinne's charms, but in the end succumbs (and who could blame him?). Eventually his foster-father, Aengus Óg, the God of Love, manages to arrange a peace with Fionn, and the couple settle down in Sligo.

It had always been foretold by the druids, however, that Diarmuid would be killed by a wild boar, and this comes to pass when he is out hunting with Fionn and the other war-riors. Fionn has the power to cure fatal wounds by giving water from his hands, but twice he lets the water flow through his fingers. He is taken to task by his grandson, Oscar, and takes up the water a third time, but now it is too late, and Diarmuid cannot be revived.

Some versions say that his body was brought to Brú na Bóinne for burial; others that Gráinne vowed eternal ven-geance through her children on Fionn. The great stones called Diarmuid and Gráinne's Bed, found all over the countryside and often marked on maps, are said to be the places where the couple snatched rest and relief in their flight from the anger of the thwarted leader.

It has long been believed that visiting one of these and lying on the stone, or even (where possible) sleeping on it, will pro-mote fertility. This formed part of early beliefs surrounding lovely Gougane Barra in West Cork. Women from ancient times up to quite recently would visit and spend the night, in the hope of successfully bearing children in the years ahead. Legend has it that King Brian Ború's wife made the pilgrimage for this purpose, since sons and heirs were essential for a leader.

Such beliefs are also attached to some sacred wells, discussed in more detail in the next chapter. Naturally enough, when Christianity began to gain power in the country (often in fact supported by local kings, who saw this new religion as a useful way to control unruly settlements – 'Sure I can't be everywhere!'), the clergy were at pains to discourage these traditions.

Today, Gougane Barra is determinedly Catholic, with a special Gougane Sunday on the last weekend in September marked by hundreds crossing the hills from all directions, coming down into the secluded valley to celebrate Mass. In the eighteenth and nineteenth centuries, these gatherings tended to descend (or ascend?) into wild revelry, and so the Church, predictably, did what it could to stamp out the joyous side of the event, to make its followers concentrate on the religious observations. And yet, it can give quite a queer feeling to stand in that valley around midday on Gougane Sunday and see the first tiny figures appear over the shoulders of the surrounding mountains, making their way along timeworn tracks down to the lake and the island below. The old ways may have been given a Christian overlay, but they are still observed.

CIRCLING THE STONES

The magic of an unending circle, so beloved of our ancient peoples. Stand in the centre of one of these strangely atmospheric rings of great grey stones and you can feel the past swirl around you like the mist that has known these rocks for millennia. As with the enormous monuments discussed above, there is no firm consensus on what purpose these might have served, what their place in the lives of the community might have been, but clearly they must have been gathering places, sites of ceremony and ritual. They may originally have been sheltered within an outer circle of a ráth or fort that has since eroded away. Often a tall central stone survives, and 'outliers' – two tall monoliths marking the outer entranceway beyond which the general attendees might not be permitted to go. The druids of ancient Ireland, of course, if one might be permitted to make use of a very modern formula, had 'access all areas' in order to carry out their important duties.

One of those duties would certainly have been the sacred ritual bonfire, created and lit on the most important festivals such as Samhain, Bealtaine or Lughnasa. Near Raphoe in Donegal, there is a wonderful hint of time-honoured customs in a battered and worn signpost pointing up a narrow track, pointing the way to 'Beltany Stone Circle'. A great ring of sixty-four ancient rocks (there would have been more, perhaps bringing the total up to around eighty), at least 4,000 years old, rounded and smoothed by the weathering of millennia, dedicated specifically to the May Day festival. What more could you want? There are vestiges of a central cairn, possibly suggesting that the stones once surrounded a tall structure or mound of some kind, used in the Bealtaine ceremonies.

A small, carved stone head dating from the Iron Age was found here, which may possibly have been a mould from which

Beltany Stone Circle in Donegal, once a scene of many rituals.

ceremonial masks were formed in bronze or even gold. It can't be seen there anymore, sadly, since it now rests securely in the vaults of the National Museum in Dublin. (It brings to mind that final scene in *Indiana Jones and the Raiders of the Lost Ark*, where the wonderful artefact is safely pushed into obscurity in a vast warehouse, there to remain presumably forever.)

Beltany Stone Circle is a stunning place to visit, sited on top of a high hill with a spectacular view all over the surrounding countryside. It is itself of course also clearly visible from many miles away, and thus was easy for worshippers or gatherers to find their way to. Not only rituals and ceremonies but also star-gazing studies, vital in the work and knowledge of the druids, would have taken place here on this raised site. The hill is packed with crystal quartzite, incidentally, which also makes it a good choice as a location for such research, as discussed earlier in this chapter. Our ancestors were watching and predicting such major events as solar and lunar eclipses, as well as the precise time the sun turned from winter to spring, a long time ago. Only thus could they wisely advise the people on the best times to plant and to reap, as well as to observe rituals. Again a reminder that these days we depend far too much on technological advances (are they really advances?) and electronic communication to interpret what the wise ones of old learned by constantly studying the skies.

Beltany is far from the main tourist trail and all the more exciting for that, since when you make your way there, you are likely to be on your own, with nobody else to interrupt your communion with the past. Take time to listen for voices, laughter and music of the Otherworld. Look for the ring and cup marks carved on some of the stones.

There are ring and cup marks to be found at Ireland's largest stone circle too, but you will have to look hard for them, in just the right light. Grange, near the excavated site of Lough Gur in Co. Limerick, is enormous, a full 45.72 metres (150 feet) in diameter and encorporating 113 stones. The largest of these stones is known as Rannach Crom Dubh, or Crom Dubh's Division, marking it as another site of veneration for the oldest harvest god, whom we met in Chapter V. As you stand directly before him, he doesn't exactly give the welcoming or warm feeling that you often find in other stone circles – indeed he is a threatening presence, warning what will happen if you fail in your pleas and he decides not to assist those all-important crops to grow to fulfilment and reaping. The Crom Dubh stone is a sobering sight in its size and grandeur, and all the more worth seeing for that. It makes us appreciate that life long, long ago was a struggle for survival, not a matter of touring around just for fun and enjoying breathtaking sights.

Uragh Stone Circle in Kerry is another lone site that takes the breath away, but this time for joy, and not just because you have to climb a steep hill to find it. Sited above a great, silent lake, with views on all sides to the surrounding hills, it's small by comparison with Beltany or Grange, but if possible even more heartstopping in its powerful atmosphere. And it is welcoming rather than intimidating, a place of happiness. Standing on the top of that hill with the tall stones as friendly companions, you gaze around and feel a surge of contentment at just being here with these ancient monoliths. How many crowded to this hilltop in former times to observe the seasonal rituals?

Another, even tinier, circle is hidden deep in the woods at Lissyvigeen (again, note the 'lios' in the name), just outside Killarney. Two huge outlier standing stones in the field beyond hint at its former importance as a ritual site. Today it is tucked away in its sheltered copse, but in past times, the track to it would have been well worn by believers.

On a hill above Castletownshend in Co. Cork stand three incredibly tall stone monoliths, the tallest over four metres. They are part of a rare layout known as a stone row, and are known generally as the Fingers. They have an almost hostile presence as you glimpse them from the road below, like watchers over the land and passers-by. Climb up, and you will find a fourth stone lying nearby. There was a fifth stone too, but, disgracefully, it was removed by a local landowner and installed at his estate in Castletownshend. Try to see the remaining three at dusk or (best of all) with the moon behind them.

Stone rows are unusual, and their purpose, although undoubtedly ritualistic, is not fully understood. In a land that favoured

The Fingers stone row on a hill above Castletownshend.

circles above all, they must have had a special purpose. Perhaps they marked a power or ley line; perhaps they pointed the way to an important site. There is a superb line known as the Sessions, near the village of Bweeng in the Boggeragh Mountains, and another, fascinatingly now only visible at low tide, near Crookhaven in West Cork. Clearly this last must once have stood on dry land, before the vagaries of tides and tectonic shifts changed the balance of sand and sea. Whatever it was built for, it holds its secrets and its memories to itself.

Visiting any of these circles, rows or monoliths, you cannot but feel the presence of Themselves, and imagine them coming out by moonlight to dance or make music. Indeed, over the centuries, it became customary for local people to gather at these sacred sites and honour the Good People by dancing around them at dawn on festival days. Of course, in equally customary fashion, the Christian Church tried its best to put a stop to such antics. Today, the tradition is being revived, thanks to the knowledge being spread again through social media. What was once instinctively known is now reawakened and shared through the most modern of means. Perhaps the Gentry smile on the new methods being used to spread the old ways?

Needless to say, the same strictures apply to these ancient megaliths as to a fairy ráth or lios. Never deface or damage them in any way, as retribution will surely follow. Many are the stories of those who so dared and were punished, and not all in the distant past either. One of the most recent is that of Sean Quinn, once Ireland's richest man. At the height of his success, he owned pubs, hotels, glass and plastics works, motor and health insurance companies, and cement, wind energy and insulation interests, not just in Ireland, but also across the UK and Europe. Unwise investments caused his ruin, say the business reports, but every knowledgeable person in his home region of Cavan knows the anger of Themselves had far more to do with it.

It was the legendary Aughrim wedge tomb near Ballyconnell, which had stood peacefully and undisturbed for at least 4,000 years, that proved his undoing. In 1992, seeking to expand a massive quarry nearby for his concrete company, Quinn found the Aughrim tomb to be very much in the way of his plans. He demanded permission from the Office of Public Works to move this protected megalith and, to their shame it must be said, they granted his request. To add insult to grievous injury, after the site was fully excavated, the ancient monument was moved, literally stone by stone, to the grounds of Quinn's new hotel on the other side of Ballyconnell.

Well, locals might say, what could you expect after such a deliberate flying in the face of the Good People? Everything turned against the tycoon. He lost one business after another, ending up with nothing. Local residents believed that he asked for trouble by moving the tomb. 'There would be a lot of people who would think you could never have any luck after that.'

(Incidentally, the same prohibition applies to graffiti scratched or sprayed on ancient monuments, or even the secret carrying away of a souvenir rock or pebble. Don't even think of it!)

A farmer near Crusheen in Co. Clare was in a bit of a fix when one of his cows, using an ancient wedge tomb as a convenient scratching post, managed to get her head jammed between the venerable stones. 'I couldn't think what to do. I know you mustn't damage them in any way. So I stood and thought for a while, and the voice came into my head as clear as you like: "Do whatever you have to in getting her free, but no more." Well, that's what I did. I got out a metal rod and a hammer, and it only took a few chips off the stone to free her. I put a fence around that wedge tomb the very same day I can tell you!'

The majority of people who care instinctively for our past and our heritage would never do anything to damage these relics of an older, wiser time, and you can see the evidence of that in so many places. Two examples: by the side of a busy road in Co. Cork, a wall has been carefully shaped to shield a venerable standing stone, not touching it, but protecting it from any possible damage. By the front gate of a city terraced house, surrounded on all sides by urban development, another standing stone still remains where it was placed many thousands of years ago. 'We wouldn't dream of doing other than caring for it,' says Noelle, who lives there. 'Even now, when we are planning an extension, that stone has to be first consideration.' Thankfully, the old beliefs live on.

An entrance to the Otherworld is believed to be hidden behind the sheer cliff face of Ben Bulben.

CHAPTER VII

HIDDEN IN THE LANDSCAPE

Megaliths, dolmens, stone circles, stone rows, pillar stones – all have their own aura of mystery and more than a strong echo of the past. These were put in place by long-ago hands, but the landscape itself has a major part to play when other fairy portals are being sought. Caves, hills and mountains, rivers, lakes, wells and trees all have their guardian nature spirits. The Good People are everywhere, as befits the protectors of our land.

WHERE DOES THIS MYSTERIOUS CAVE LEAD?

It is natural that caves, with their dark and mysterious circular openings, are also seen as entrances to the Otherworld, and they have in consequence amassed many legends, accounts of what might be found by those courageous enough to explore beyond those foreboding thresholds. Always remember, however, that caves pose a risk, and in the case of some, considerable danger. A sudden downpour can hugely increase the flow of water through such labyrinthine passages. Don't take any chances.

One of the most famous fairy caves, long believed to be an entrance to the Otherworld, and with references going back to ancient times, is Oweynagat, or the Cave of the Cat. It lies near the splendid site of Rathcroghan in Co. Roscommon, said to have been the royal fort of Queen Maeve (she who caused the great Cattle Raid of Cooley, immortalised in the epic poem Táin Bó Cuailnge.) The cave itself, in contrast to the excellent visitor-oriented Rathcroghan, is quite a tiny affair, and some distance away from it along country lanes. You need to book with the visitor centre and be taken there by a guide. Given that the entrance is small and the space inside fairly limited, it is probably not an ideal place for those inclined to claustrophobia or who find it difficult to manoeuvre in cramped conditions.

Is it worth it? Oh yes. Creepy, uncomfortable, distinctly stressful, but an experience you won't forget. There is a superb ogham stone used as a lintel just inside the entrance, indicating that our forefathers had no worries about utilising one ancient monument to prop up another which they perceived of greater importance. Translated, the enigmatic short carved lines read: 'Fraech son of Medb', giving further substance to the belief that nearby Rathcroghan really was the centre of Maeve's kingdom.

It is called the Cave of the Cat because it was believed that the Morrigan, the dreaded warlike goddess, used this as her entrance to our world. She would emerge in the shape of a large black cat with huge green eyes that fixed you with a threatening glare. Tales are also told of terrifying three-headed pigs that would come bursting out of the cave and lay waste all around them; also an interesting story of 'saffron-coloured birds', equally bent on destruction. Needless to say, the Christian Church frowned on stories involving the old pagan goddesses. The cave was rechristened the Gateway to Hell, in hopes of thereby discouraging those who followed the earlier beliefs. It didn't work. Oweynagat is still much visited today, although not everyone makes the effort to struggle through the entrance.

Big black cats, three-headed pigs, threatening saffron birds – enough to put you off? But here is a personal experience that shows another side to the Good People and their animal manifestations – believe it or dismiss it as coincidence as you will.

We had gone down into the cave, Richard and I, to get the feel of the place and to take some photographs by flash. Having admired the ogham stone lintel and looked around the cramped space, I felt it was time to extricate myself again, while my devoted photographer husband took several more shots. Easier said than done – you can wriggle downwards fairly easily, but it's a lot more difficult to wriggle upwards. Halfway up, still caught between one world and the other, pinned between unyielding rocks, stress was beginning to make itself felt. And at that moment, I caught the sound of soft, comforting purring, right in my ear. 'I've really lost it now,' I thought, putting it down to fevered imagination. But the purring continued, and as I managed to pull myself higher, and my shoulders at last got into the open air, I was able to turn my head to see that a small, white cat was sitting right beside me, purring encouragingly.

Clambering out, I looked back in disbelief; it was still there. Richard emerged a few minutes later and was able to take the

pictures that proved the incident. The guide from Rathcroghan couldn't explain it, except to say it must have come from a farm some distance down the lane. Very likely. But it was there, and just when it was most needed. That's not something you forget.

The Burren, that amazing rocky landscape in Co. Clare, is of course honeycombed with caves, as limestone regions usually are. One of the most famous is Pollnagollum, which may just have given JRR Tolkien the name for one of his most infamous characters. Tolkien loved this part of Ireland and knew it well from many visits. On one occasion, a friend took him to Pollnagollum, a very far-reaching network of caves formed by underground rivers coursing through the soft limestone. If you know your Hobbit, you will remember that Bilbo comes across Gollum in just such a confusing, dark and damp world of labyrinthine passages and black lakes. There is every reason to believe that Tolkien was thinking of his summers in the Burren and the resonance of the name of that cave when he sat at his desk in Oxford and penned that legendary work.

If you visit Pollnagollum, remember the warning we gave earlier. This cave complex is particularly susceptible to sudden floodings, with high levels of rainwater rushing through the worn passageways to trap unwary speleologists. Don't go without a guide, and keep a sharp eye to the weather forecast if and when you do. But even the sight of the daunting entrance, down in a steep pit surrounded by rowan trees, is dramatic enough for most visitors.

There are, in fact, several other caves called Pollnagollum in Ireland – the name means 'pigeon hole' and refers to their usually small, circular entrances, which doubtless add to the sense of mystery and fear surrounding them. One such is a cavern located between Lough Corrib and Lough Mask, just outside of the village of Cong (where they filmed *The Quiet Man*, by the way). As is usual, a subterranean stream runs through it, but less usually, it is said to be home to a fairy trout. Obviously, any attempt to catch this trout would be highly inadvisable, since it would certainly annoy Themselves. But according to legend, one soldier in bygone times succeeded, only to be horrified when the fish spoke to him. It warned him of the consequences of his actions, and commanded that it be returned to the stream forthwith. Which command he duly obeyed. Sensible fellow.

Kesh Corann, a fairy mountain in Sligo, is possessed of many dramatic cave entrances, curving out of the sheer rock face that towers above a wide valley. There are many myths and legends concerning this mountain, the earliest dealing with Corann, skilled harpist to Dian Cécht, the wonderful god of healing and son of the Daghda. A huge enchanted sow (Caelceis by

The caves of Kesh on Keshcorran Hill, said to be a home of the Good People.

name) was running wild throughout the countryside, causing great destruction (I wonder if she was related to that savage spirit pig roosting in Co. Cork whom we met in Chapter V?). Eventually, a royal hunting party set out from Brú na Bóinne to find and destroy her. Instead, she killed many of the party's warriors along the way, until Corann's enchanted music subdued her. The remaining warriors were finally able to finish off the beast, and its great body became the hill of Kesh Corann. Since then, the mountain has always been associated with the Tuatha dé Danann, and it is strongly believed that they still inhabit the caves of Kesh.

You can climb to the caves, and venture inside a little way if you dare, but there is always the risk that you might go too far and not be able to find your way back. If you hear strains of ethereal music when beyond the reach of daylight, it could well be Corann stroking the strings of his magical harp. Listen too long and you may never wish to return to the human world.

One of the strangest caves in Ireland, historically speaking, must be that which lies hidden under the Christian pilgrimage site of Lough Derg in Donegal. This naturally circular island in its mysterious, shadowy lake has been revered as a place of worship for many centuries, and indeed was marked on some of the earliest maps. Prior to the Church of Rome arriving onstage, it is very likely to have been a sacred site devoted to the older gods of our land.

Underneath the island itself was a concealed cave, where those who wished to experience the Otherworld could spend the night if they dared. It seems that there were strange currents of air and vapours within this cave, which caused hallucinations and visions of a world beyond. (One is reminded of the legendary Oracle of Delphi, who is said to have resided on a stone placed across a deep volcanic crevasse. Inhaling the vapours that arose, she thereby remained in a constantly confused state of

The island of Lough Derg – would you know there was a cave underneath?

mind, which rendered her foretellings exceptionally difficult of interpretation. 'Delphic utterances' is a well-known expression, meaning convoluted or cryptic messages.)

Naturally enough, the new and enthusiastic religion stamped heavily on the old pagan beliefs, and the cave on the island at Lough Derg was blocked up. Over the ensuing centuries, they enthusiastically built properly approved religious structures. And continued to build. Today, the enormous basilica covers the entire surface of the small island, with not a hint of that secret cave lying beneath. It's presumably still there, but not likely to be accessible again in many lifetimes. Wouldn't you like to see it, though? Is there – just perhaps – a ferociously guarded secret flagstone set with an iron ring, hidden in the depths of the lowest crypt of the basilica? The clergy certainly aren't saying. And the many pilgrims who throng here each summer to spend days and nights in penitential exercises do not have any idea what secrets might lie far below in the lost cave. That their exhausting circles of the island, often bare-foot, and their prescribed prayers, chanted in specific num-bers, are descended from ancient pagan rituals is not an idea that occurs to them. Why should it? The Church has claimed them for its own, and taken such magical numbers as three, seven and nine into its ownership.

THERE WITHIN THE HILLS THEY DWELL

The Good People are known to maintain their splendid palace forts within our rounded hills and mountains too, usu-ally behind great towering walls of stone. If you arrive at an opportune moment, you just may see a gleam of light from behind the bare face of the rock, or hear the faint strains of Otherworld music. Up in Sligo, they have long held that the steeper side of towering Ben Bulben holds a secret entrance to just such a place; the same is said of Slieve Mish in Kerry. The much-loved children's writer Patricia Lynch wrote several books about a leprechaun named Brogeen who lives in the Fort of Sheen on the side of Slieve Mish, but often slips out to enjoy himself among the people of the human world. In *Brogeen and the Princess of Sheen*, he follows a young spirit girl who wants to experience this world for herself. Of course it isn't anything like she has been used to, and Brogeen has a busy time trying to rescue her from the dangers and setbacks she inevitably encounters as her arrogant fairy ways anger those she meets who only want to help this lost child.

Most visitors to Ireland who are keen to see all they can of our ancient heritage will visit the Hill of Tara. This has always been a Celtic inauguration site for kings, rather than a powerful spiritual place. There are innumerable mounds and rings from successive ages now buried underneath those still visible today, but as yet they are only to be seen by advanced underground scanning. Though the tall pillar stone at the summit of the hill is claimed as the Lia Fáil, or Stone of Destiny, in fact it isn't. That powerful flagstone was taken out of this country thousands of years ago, and is now celebrated as the English Stone of Scone (pronounced 'skoon' by the way). It is placed underneath the royal throne in London when a new king or queen is crowned.

Well, how did that happen? It seems that Fergus, ruler of the kingdom of Dal Riada (which spanned Northern Ireland and a sizeable piece of neighbouring Scotland), unwisely lent our inauguration stone to his brother, who was being crowned in a Scottish kingdom. And what happens when you lend something? That's right – you rarely get it back. The stone, with all its magical associations (it is said to cry aloud in triumph if the right ruler places his foot on it, to remain silent if it is a usurper), stayed in Scotland thereafter until the English snatched it in one of their attempts to establish firm command over their unruly northern neighbour. In London it remained until as recently as 1996. Then, after much discussion, it was returned to Scotland, and kept in Edinburgh Castle with the Honours of Scotland. It is still claimed as the property of the British Crown, however, and is transported to London for use at coronations.

The tall stone you see at Tara today is said to have been erected in the 1820s by locals, in memory of the many who died in the area during the 1798 rebellion. PW Joyce, the eminent historian of the early twentieth century, claimed to have spoken to a man half a century earlier who had actually been involved in putting up that later monolith, which had been found lying flat in a ditch below the hill.

Joyce, in his *The Wonders of Ireland* (1911), makes a very valid further point:

> *… the coronation stones used so generally by the Gaelic tribes all over Ireland and Scotland, were comparatively small and portable, like that now under the Coronation Chair at Westminster which is a flag 25 inches by 15 inches by 9 inches thick. But the present pillar-stone at Tara is 12 feet long by nearly 2 feet in diameter. It would be very unsuitable for standing on during the ceremonies of installation and coronation.*

Still, it can't be denied that it looks dramatic (and eminently photographable) standing nobly up there, looking down over the spreading countryside all around. To find the real home of the Otherworld, however, the place where the most ancient rituals and ceremonies took place, you need to move further inland, to the fabled Hill of Uisneach in Co. Westmeath. This, in our oldest mythology, is definitively the sacred centre of Ireland, the very home of gods like the Daghda and Lugh. It was, from the earliest times, a place of assembly where learned druids held their rituals. There are suggestions too, in scarce sources, that wise men and women from other faraway lands came here for such famous ceremonies, especially that at Bealtaine, sailing up the Shannon and then by a tributary river right to Uisneach. Oh, to go back in time and see those boats of ancient days moving up our great river to attend these gatherings.

The Stone of Divisions or Catstone, at the Hill of Uisneach.

There was a *bile* or sacred tree here (nowadays, there is so much tree cover, it is hard to know what type it was, but probably oak or ash), under which ceremonies were carried out. More importantly, there was, and still is, a sacred rock, the Ail na Míreann, or Stone of the Divisions. This was held to be the *omphalos*, or central point of Ireland, the meeting place between this and the Otherworld. Today, this rock is more familiarly referred to as the Catstone, since some have fancied a resemblance to the face of a cat in its surface.

Great ritual fires were lit on Uisneach at Bealtaine and Samhain, and happily, this ancient tradition has been revived in recent years, with social media as the ideal means of spreading the word. Enthusiastic people come from all corners of the country to move among the megaliths, holy wells and ringforts, which are everywhere.

Uisneach was linked to Tara by the ancient way known as the Slighe Assail. The modern R392 follows most of its route, so if you plan to use that regional road, you can revel in the knowledge that you are following one of the oldest ways in Ireland.

Is this a fairy path?

Speaking of old ways and tracks, we should not forget the fairy paths. These are the regular routes followed by the Good People as they travel around, and They do not take kindly to finding them blocked or altered. Often these paths link two ráths or lios that are within sight of one another. However, they are not usually visible to our limited human eyes. You might, on very close examination, notice a tiny pathway worn in the grass along a hedge, or a minuscule track going over a ditch or bank. The disbeliever will immediately say, 'Oh, that's just an animal track,' but it's always possible that it's a fairy path. In any case, Themselves would never mind sharing their roadway with a field mouse or a hedgehog. (If they weren't putting on that disguise themselves anyway, which is also always possible.) Michael Moore of Killyfargy, Co. Monaghan, recorded a traditional way of establishing whether spirit routes might be disturbed by human building.

Our house was taken down because it was in the path of the fairies and placed here. The people long ago before they would build a house would stick down rods in the ground for a few nights where they were going to build the house. If the rods were tossed or pulled up this was considered by the people that the place they were about to build the house was on the path of the fairies. The Maguires of Carn before they built their house placed rods in several places and every night they would be lifted. At last the Maguires put down the rods where their house now stands and strange to say they were never touched.

Another interesting story comes from Kildallan, Co. Westmeath:

There is a path known as the fairies' path up near Milltown, and there are two houses built on this path. There was a fair in Ballynacargy on the first of April, and the boys in one of these homes happened to be going to the fair the following morning. Some of their relatives remained up late to call them early for the fair. At twelve o'clock they could hear great rumbling noises

Is this a fairy path in the frosty grass?

about the place, and when they called the boys later, they said it must be the fairies passing through the house on their way down to the other house on the path.

After some time the noise died away, but at three it returned just as strong as before, and it is said the fairies were going back again to the cave at the back of the house after visiting the other fairies.

The interest here lies in the fact that the two lads take the disturbances for granted, as a normal occurrence.

In many cases, if a human habitation did happen to be blocking the path for Themselves, a less radical solution than levelling the property was to leave a door or window always open on each end of the house. The Good People could thus continue on their way without check or hindrance, and the risk of their anger would be lessened. Where a new building was contemplated, however, it was (and still is) advisable to check by using the rods or sticks method indicated above. After all, you would always make sure of your foundations, wouldn't you? And possible claims by neighbouring landowners? Well then, why not ancient rights of way?

Fairy paths should never be blocked, intentionally or otherwise. In the nineteenth century, Lady Carbery of Castlefreke in Co. Cork decided to establish a 'sprigging' or lacemaking school in the nearby village of Rathbarry, to give employment to needy local people. An excellent scheme and very worthwhile. However, the site she chose, on the edge of a wood, was highly inadvisable. Local people told her straight away that it was on a known fairy path, and that her school should on no account be placed there. She was obstinate, said it was by far the best location and insisted on going ahead. She had to push the building work, since local labourers weren't too happy to be involved in either the digging or the construction, but finally she got it done. The school prospered for some time, and beautiful pieces of lacework were created, but when the market failed, the school fell into disuse. Lady Carbery then kindly offered the building to a local homeless man, but he refused to take advantage of the gift, saying it had been built across that fairy path and no luck would come to him if he lived there.

You can still see the little white building today, on the out-skirts of Rathbarry, beautifully maintained as a tourist attrac-tion, with lace curtains at the windows to denote its original use. If you do go, don't omit to walk the woodland path behind the former school as well, and perhaps leave a sprig of flowers or heather under a tree as an offering to Themselves. And always listen to local advice if thinking of building or otherwise chang-ing some untouched environment. You'll be told quick enough if there is a fairy path there.

Country children have always loved pretending that a natu-ral hollow in a tree is really the entry to an imaginative world. They will decorate its mossy entrance, place acorns or hazelnuts outside, even make tiny ladders or miniature stone steps for access. A relatively recent craze has seen brightly coloured 'fairy doors' placed at the foot of tree trunks, along woodland paths, or even in special park layouts for tourists with names like the Fairy Glen or the Fairy Village. Commercial outlets were quick to jump on that particular bandwagon, and you can now get all shapes and sizes of these imaginative entries to the Other-world. They can be a bit garish if found in large numbers in an otherwise natural environment, but one can see them as repre-senting a genuine desire or even need to have such evidence of an alternative existence, of Tír na nÓg. This is not just among children, but adults too, wearying perhaps of the stresses of our ultra-modern world. Who would not wish to escape through that door into a wonderland full of magic, just for a while?

The sprigging school at Rathbarry
– was this built across a fairy path?

TOUCH NOT THE FAIRY TREE

Like those imaginary mossy doors, fairy paths are often present in woods and forests, even if not clearly visible. The trees themselves are very much part of the Otherworld too, with their own guardian nature spirits. In the great days of the Brehon laws, before the coming of Christianity and, later, the enforced replacement of our own legal system by the alien British system, this was fully recognised. Trees were revered and given their own status and classification with a scheme of recompense for damage, unwitting or otherwise. To dig up or kill a growing tree was a very serious offence, while even breaking a branch was punishable. (A humane provision, however, allowed the starving passer-by to steal a handful of nuts or apples if really needed.)

Trees under Brehon law were divided into noble, common, shrub and bramble, with the nobles of the wood being oak, hazel, holly, yew, ash, Scots pine and apple. (Fuller discussion of this can be found in our *Brehon Laws: The ancient wisdom of Ireland*, O'Brien Press, 2020.)

Strangely enough, though, although all trees were valued and cared for in ancient Ireland, the most notable and venerated is not the mighty oak or the yew, but the relatively small and bushy hawthorn. Also called whitethorn, for the wonderful display of scented blossom it throws across the countryside in the month of May, it is better known in every corner of the land as 'the fairy tree', very much protected by our nature spirits as well as acting as a portal to the Otherworld. It is treated with enormous respect, and damaging it is believed to bring very bad luck indeed. That is why you will often see one standing proudly right in the middle of a huge field of ripening barley or oats, untouched and carefully avoided by heavy ploughing or threshing machinery. No farmer would think of moving it.

Another trees with strong links to the Otherworld is the rowan or mountain ash. Druids slept on beds of rowan branches, that their dreams might be the clearer; and to decide the answer to a complex problem, rowan wands inscribed with ogham symbols were cast, the way they fell being noted and interpreted accordingly. (The same practice is observed in China with yarrow stalks.) Both this tree with its rich bounty of scarlet berries, and the crab apple that gifts the autumn with its hedgerow crop of little fruits (bitter to eat but excellent as jelly), are gifts of the nature spirits. It's a good idea to plant them as protectors in the hedges that surround your home. They will discourage any passing evil from entering your safe place.

In ancient times, each important settlement also had its own bile or sacred tree, usually a strong, tall, aged one like an oak, ash, beech or yew. Here local assemblies would be held, and minor disputes settled. To damage a bile was unthinkable, punished by expulsion from the community or even the dreaded penalty of being sent 'beyond the ninth wave' in a boat without oar or rudder, to be dealt with by the gods as they saw fit. In later generations, when the old laws had perforce to yield to the new ones imposed by England, the Good People continued the tradition of protecting their sacred trees, as this story from the Mayo of the 1930s shows:

There was once a man called Peter Tiernan living in Huntsfield. A tall ash tree grew in his land. The people called it Crann Mór, the Great Tree, and they used to say it belonged to the fairies. One day Peter went out to cut wood and he was in a great hurry so he cut a few branches off Crann Mór. When he had enough cut and coming home he met an old woman that looked like a beggar woman. 'Good day Mam,' said Peter. 'Good day,' said she, 'you'll be very sorry yet for interfering with Crann Mór. You had better leave the wood back again.' 'Well,' said Peter, 'don't I want a bit of a fire?' 'All right,' said she, 'go on.' With that the woman disappeared. When Peter went home he burned the wood and a few days after that one of his best cows died. After she died the people skinned her, and every blow that Peter gave Crann Mór, they were plain to be seen in the cow's flesh. About in a fortnight after that, Peter was going out to the haggard for hay and he saw the very same cow eating from one of the haycocks, so from that day till this Crann Mór was left alone.

But then, all trees are beloved of the Good People, and it is our responsibility and charge to treat every one of them thoughtfully. If a tree chances to stand by a sacred well or other site believed to have associations with Themselves, then you will see rags, ribbons, scraps of wool and other tokens tied carefully to the branches, in pursuit of a petition or wish. These are known as 'rag trees' or 'clootie bushes' ('clootie' means cloth). There is a fine one on the side of the Hill of Tara, to take just one well-known example, and another by Creevykeel court tomb at Cliffoney above Sligo town, but you will find them by

A rag tree at Creevykeel megalithic tomb.

most healing wells or fairy mounds. Try not to leave a plastic token if you do – make it something natural like cotton, wool or wood.

The old wise ones recognised the importance of trees in maintaining a healthy environment (something we are only slowly getting back to realising today) and believed that specific nature deities cared for them. In *The Lord of the Rings*, Tolkien created ents, those wonderful, huge figures, resembling ancient trees themselves, who made caring for them their lives' work. His mention of the long-absent entwives echoes Frazer's allusion to 'woodwives' in *The Golden Bough* (that wide-ranging comparative study of different beliefs and religions, first published in 1890) and also reflects the long-held belief in Ireland that nature spirits inhabit every tree.

Definitely the most famous of our powerful trees though is the hawthorn or 'fairy bush', a scíog in Irish, known to be beloved of the Good People and never on any account to be damaged. Stories of what happens to those who wilfully and knowingly disobey tradition and damage or even dig up fairy trees are plentiful. Here are a few examples, the first from Co. Monaghan:

Another feature in this locality which the people refrain from interfering with is the 'lone bush'. One or more of these are usually seen in the middle of a field or somewhere in the open but sometimes they are in line with the ditch and they can easily be distinguished from the other bushes by being much taller. They are supposed to afford shelter to the fairies and although they cause inconvenience when they are situated in an open field that is being ploughed, still most people are inclined to put up with the inconvenience sooner than cut them down.

There was this farmer in Lougheske, he cut a fairy bush for a roost for his hens, and next morning the hens were all dead.

One day Owen Griffin went to cut a bush to put in a gap. He first cut the hanging branches and then started to cut the tree, but the hatchet was taken out of his hand and he never saw it again.

There is a fairy fort on the townland of Aughagad … Any person who ever as much as cut a bush or rod from this fort never was much the better. They either lost cattle or something happened to themselves.

Almost every fairy fort you discover will have at least one if not a whole surround of hawthorn trees on its circular banks. In the month of May, the sweetly scented blossom turns the countryside into a true fairyland, like snow in summer. This is the one time it is acceptable to cut branches of the flowering may bush and fasten them over the doors of houses and stables, to protect all within from any passing evil spirit. In past centuries, young men and women would make May Eve an occasion to go out into the woods and fields and celebrate all night, bringing home blossoming branches in the morning. For the rest of the year, those bushes must be left strictly alone.

There was once a man who was very fond of visiting and cardplaying. One night about half past twelve when he was returning from a neighbouring house, a man came out before him and spread a white table-cloth before him to have a game of cards. The man said he would and after a few hours the man got up to go home. The fairy told him he would bring him home.

The fairy took a large lamp from his pocket and told the man to follow him. The man kept following the light until he brought him to a little house under a bush. Then the fairy put out the light and asked him why did he cut the bush that was growing at the bottom of his field. The man said, 'It was in my way.' 'Well,' said the fairy, 'you are in my way too,' and he kicked him away from the house, and the man kept walking up and down and could not find his way until he turned his cap inside out and as soon as he did he found himself walking on the road in front of his own house.

The key to the importance of the hawthorn is that it is very much a 'come by chance' tree, choosing for itself where it will root and grow. In that, it is more like a cat than a dog – whereas a faithful hound will obediently go where you tell it to, a cat will choose for itself, and no command or request from you will make it change its mind. So it is with the hawthorn, and it is considered very bad luck indeed to dig one up if it happens to be in the way of whatever you are planning.

Sometimes you can get away with it if it is right in the middle of your garden (they like popping up in places like that), where there is the option of carefully taking it up and planting it with respect and apologies and best wishes in a surrounding hedge. If it accepts your apologies, it will strengthen the protection of that hedge and continue to guard against evil spirits. Just remember though that the root of a hawthorn is about three times that which is visible above the ground, so you do have to do this fairly quickly after you first spot it. Outside the garden, leave it well alone. It has chosen to be there, it has its own personal nature spirit, and they both know what they are doing.

The belief that you should never interfere with a thorn tree is as strong today as is the conviction that fairy forts are not to be meddled with. A recent proof of this occurred in 1999, when the section of the motorway from Limerick to Galway passing Newmarket-on-Fergus in Co. Clare was being constructed. A tough little hawthorn tree stood right in its path. Eddie Lenihan, a renowned local folklorist and shanachie, warned against removing that tree, reminding the developers that it would bring the worst of bad luck.

At first he was ignored. Then the story got around: first through the local newspapers, then national publications, and then the *New York Times*. Finally, to use a modern phrase, it 'went viral' – media from all over the world, as well as concerned individuals and interest groups, jumped in delightedly

The fairy tree that moved the M18 motorway in Co. Clare – the sudden bend in the road is evident.

to voice their opposition. Eventually the developers had to give in (with much annoyance, one would imagine) and alter their already well-polished plans a bit. Today, the thorn tree stands calmly and quietly at the edge of a slip road, while the tarmac speedway roars past a safe distance away on a slight but visible outward bend. Instinctive belief won out that time, over huge commercial and developmental pressure.

Even big business isn't immune to Their wrath. In the early 1980s, the car manufacturer DeLorean decided to build a new luxury car plant in Dunmurry, near Belfast. Only trouble was, a fine little hawthorn tree was standing right in the middle of the proposed site. After his workers refused to bulldoze it, chairman John DeLorean did it himself. The company subsequently went into receivership and closed for good in 1982. Short business life, long Otherworld memories.

The unwritten law against interfering with the thorn tree would seem to be as strong as ever still, then. 'Oh yes,' said a farmer up in Co. Clare last summer. 'That fairy fort over there, I have a neighbour went out to cut some kindling from the thorn trees around it, although he was warned not to. Well, he got these dreadful sores all over his hands and up his arms. Of course he brought the kindling back as quickly as possible, but it took weeks to heal the sores. Themselves don't think it's enough to say you're sorry, you see. They put a bad luck on you, and you have to endure it until they think you've paid what's due.'

Finally, and most engagingly, golfers at the Ormeau golf course in Belfast are actively encouraged to nod respectfully to the fairy tree that stands there, and apologise if they chance to hit it. Not even the club's busy gardeners are allowed to touch it. The old ways endure.

> *All night around the thorn tree the little people play,*
> *And men and women passing will turn their heads away.*
> *But if your heart's a child's heart, and if your eyes are clean,*
> *You need never fear the thorn tree that grows beyond Clogheen.*
> (Traditional)

THE POWER OF WATER

Water is essential to life, and has long been regarded as blessed when it emerges magically from the ground or flows generously from the hills to irrigate the land and the crops. The larger rivers had their own goddesses (still do); individual wells or springs were venerated; lakes were given offerings to ensure their cooperation in keeping human life going. We are on one side of the water, i.e. above, and cannot easily pass to the other side, below, and this fact links bodies of water to the Otherworld and its nature spirits. The Good People, of course, can pass naturally from one to the other with no effort at all.

The mighty River Boyne in Co. Meath, which flows by the megalithic complex of Brú na Bóinne, was, for our forefathers, an enchanted waterway by which the spirits of the dead could enter the Otherworld. It is guarded by the goddess Boann, who, as you may recall from the previous chapter, united with the Daghda to produce Aengus Óg, the god of love. She it is who sometimes appears to the people of her region in the form of a white cow. If she is generously inclined, she may send a fairy cow or two – always white with red ears – to live on a farm for a while and benefit the lucky recipient. Some legends hold that Boann demands human sacrifice every year, but this belief most likely arises from the unfortunate fact that accidents and drownings do tend to occur wherever there is a fast-flowing waterway.

The mighty Shannon is watched over by Sionann, the beautiful granddaughter of Manannán Mac Lir, god of the sea. Legend has it that she unwisely sought out the Well of Knowledge, which is said to be the source of our principal river, and ate of the nuts from the hazel trees that droop over it. The well, angered at her temerity, rose up and flooded, thus creating the great waterway that we see today. Sionann, however, being a goddess, did not die, but lived on as the river's guardian.

The Lee in Co. Cork has an interesting legend. Today it is firmly linked to St Finbarr, who founded his monastery at its source in Gougane Barra, but that's the Christian version. Nearer the truth would be the belief that Finbarr journeyed into the mountains to study at a famed druidic centre on the island in Gougane Barra's lake. Only later did he decide to change to the newer religion from Rome, but brought with him all the old knowledge and magic that he had learned here in the hills.

The Christian version of Finbarr's legend also says that he discovered a dreadful monster lurking in the lake at Gougane. He threw it out with such force that it went all the way to Lough Allua (not more than a few miles actually as the dragon flies, although the winding road quadruples that distance), where, it is said, it still lingers. The old families of Gougane, however, maintain that the monster never left, but still bides his time beneath the lake's black waters. So he is a guardian spirit of a kind, if not the beautiful and kindly one that you might expect in such a wonderful place. Still, maybe he is misunderstood, and just needs a sympathetic ear to hear his side of the highly biased tale?

All rivers and streams in Ireland have their own guardian spirits. They watch constantly to ensure that we, the thoughtless human beings, do nothing to pollute or restrict their free-flowing magical waters. Linger in such places, enjoy the peace and calm, never damage or pollute, even clear up after less thoughtful visitors, and you may see Them smile.

LO, THE MYSTERIOUS LAKE

Lakes have always been regarded as magical places, with secrets hidden beneath their waters. Many have been used over the millennia as centres of worship, with offerings being thrown into their depths to appease or petition the Good People.

Lake Muskry in the Glen of Aherlow, for example, only reached by a fairly strenuous uphill hike, was formerly known as Lough Béal Sead (Lake of the Jewel Mouth). Legend tells that the lake was once home to beautiful maidens who, every second year, became beautiful birds wearing glittering, jewelled necklaces. It was also, more threateningly, known as the Lake of the Dragon's Mouth, suggesting that yet another of the monsters banished by St Patrick lurked here. It is fairly certain that this was a site of ritual pilgrimages in ancient times, with who knows what treasures cast into its silent waters as offerings to the gods.

Lough Leane in Killarney is said to be guarded by the White Knight, who emerges from its waters every seven years to ride around the perimeter and see that all is well. Since Lough Leane is close by Muckross House, a popular place to visit, you might just be lucky enough to glimpse this ghostly rider on his white horse. To maximise your chances, you should probably walk by its waters at dusk. Just don't get locked in when they shut the gates before dark!

It was from Lough Leane that Niamh of the Golden Hair, a beautiful goddess of the Otherworld, emerged to tempt Oisín, son of Fionn Mac Cumhaill, away with her to Tír na nÓg, the Land of Youth. Mounted on a white horse with golden harness, she was so beautiful that he agreed to go with her for a short visit. In the Otherworld, however, time is not as we know it, and what seems like a brief period can be a very long time indeed. Oisín had wonderful experiences there, but one day chanced to see the simplest of reminders – a piece of ordinary wood from his own world, probably the oar from a boat, floating by the shores of a lake. Suddenly he remembered his former life, and told Niamh he must return, if only briefly, to see his comrades once more. She resisted, but eventually gave in, seeing that he was resolute. Only, she warned him, do not dismount from your horse while you are there, or the consequences will be terrible. Then she showed him the way back to the human world.

He found it oddly changed, and could not find any of his old comrades. When he met a group of men trying ineffectually to move a large boulder, he couldn't resist reaching down to show them how a strong hero manages such simple tasks. The saddle girth broke, he fell to the ground and was instantly an old old man, dying before their eyes. Those who are taken to the Otherworld can rarely return unscathed to the life they knew before.

Several lakes in Kerry are said to be haunted by dreadful monsters, according to the Dublin writer WR Le Fanu (brother of the better-known author of Gothic horror, Sheridan Le Fanu). In *Seventy Years of Irish Life* (1893), he wrote:

That dreadful beast, the Wurrum – half-fish, half-dragon – still survives in many a mountain lake – seldom seen, indeed, but often heard. Near our fishing quarters in Kerry there are two such lakes, one the beautiful lake at the head of the

Blackwater River, called Lough Brin, or Bran as he is now called, the dreadful wurrum which inhabits it. The man who minds the boats there speaks with awe of Bran; he tells me he has never seen him and hopes he never may.

Apparently, this monster is still glimpsed from time to time at Lough Brin, so if you are up in those remote Kerry hills keep an eye out – but not from too close to the shore!

The people of Belcarra, Co. Mayo, have a frightening story to tell of a lake monster that terrorised the area back in the 1920s:

Situated between Knockmore and Balla lies a very remark-able lake, having no outlet of any kind. Although small, the lake is very deep and is supposed to have no bottom.

A large Eel dwells in this lake, people call it the Master Eel. This Eel is supposed to be able to turn himself into the form of any animal.

Old people not long dead have seen the Eel come grazing on Knockmore hills, in the form of a calf, pig or donkey. Others have seen him put his tail into his mouth and let a whistle loud enough to be heard for miles around, and immediately afterwards there was a terrible rushing and lashing of the waters in the lake followed a minute after by perfect calmness of the waters. Up to the present day no fishing is done on this lake, as people say it is unlucky to interfere with it in any way.

The narrator says her brothers heard the awful whistle.

Lough Brin, said to hold a dreadful monster.

There are magical lakes known as 'turloughs' in various parts of Ireland, which can appear and disappear at will. Usually this happens in an area mostly composed of limestone, where water will sink underground when levels are low, only to appear, almost miraculously, when rainfall raises the level once more. Naturally enough, though, interference by Themselves is always suspected.

Then there is the Lake of the Fairy Badger up in Clare. That fearsome creature sallies forth at night and snatches children, small animals and anything else that may be about. Many other lakes have their own legends attached, often to do with lurking monsters. The water kelpie though, a form of aquatic horse that snatches unwary passers-by, common enough in neighbouring Scotland, is rarely seen in Irish lakes. We apparently prefer our wurrums. And why not? Do guardian spirits always have to be tall, noble and beautiful? Can't a serpent or a dragon do an equally good job of protecting what is of ancient importance?

(You hardly need reminding that any mention of a serpent or dragon in Ireland is always a clue to concentrated effort on the part of the Christian Church to expunge the old ways and the old traditions. This is thus also a clue to the likelihood that the specific location was a sacred place for millennia before their arrival.)

Lough Neagh near Belfast is the largest lake in either the British Isles or Ireland, being surrounded by five of the six counties of Northern Ireland (only Fermanagh doesn't have a toe in the water). Its name in Irish is Loch nEachach, Eachaid being another name for the great god the Daghda. Its creation is explained in many legends: one tells of how the giant Fionn Mac Cumhaill hauled up a great handful of earth and hurled it across the sea at a giant in Scotland with whom he had a dispute. The earth landed in the sea and became the Isle of Man, while the hollow left behind filled with water and became Lough Neagh.

Another legend claims that the lough came into being through the carelessness of a servant girl at the royal palace that once stood here, who was charged with guarding the king's well of fresh water. This well had to be kept covered at all times, but one evening she was distracted by the crying of her child and went to soothe it, leaving the lid open. The water burst forth, drowning the kingdom and everyone in it, and became the lake we see today. Tradition says that from time to time in the right conditions, you can see the domes and spires of that lost palace gleaming beneath the surface.

> *On Lough Neagh's bank, as the fisherman strays*
> *When the clear cold eve's declining.*
> *He sees the round towers of other days*
> *In the waves beneath him shining.*
> (Thomas Moore, 'Let Erin Remember')

Much the same legend is told of the Lough in the centre of Cork city, an unusual place to find a natural body of water, although it is much appreciated by all who live around it (as well as by wildfowl, which gather here each winter in great numbers). Here lived a king called Corc, who had a wonderful spring by his palace that gave fresh, pure water to all who wanted it. The king, however, became possessive and built a wall around the source, covering it with a strong, heavy, locked lid, so that nobody else could benefit from it but himself and his chosen guests. At a great banquet, he sent his daughter, Fíoruisce (the name means Spring Water), to fetch the treasured liquid, and a handsome prince accompanied her on the errand. Now, one source says she fell into the well and he dived to rescue her, but both were drowned. Another version claims they were dallying while fetching the water, and quite forgot to close the lid, with the same consequences.

Corkman John Spillane, singer/songwriter and composer of Irish music, recently completed a mammoth task

The Lough in Cork is said to hold a drowned city.

that demonstrates his passion for our old legends as well as our landscape. *Fíoruisce – The Legend of the Lough* is nothing less than an entire folk opera based on this well-loved story (which you can discover at fioruisce.ie).

'It's my magnum opus,' John admits freely. 'Like the several underground streams that feed the Lough of Cork, this project happens in a place that brings together my love of myth, music, the Irish language, storytelling and a great love of the Lough itself. This local legend turns out to be a powerful myth concerning enclosure, water rights and the very formation of the landscape. We are incredibly rich in these legends of the past and it is so important to value them, to pass them on to the next generation and the one after that.'

And does he believe there is some truth in the legend? 'Well, why not?' he replies. 'Go down there yourself at sunset one evening and see if you can spot the spires and towers of that drowned palace. If you have the belief, then see them you will.'

CAN THIS WELL HELP ME?

The fresh water of springs and wells, bubbling up naturally from the earth itself and so essential for survival, has at all times been valued, indeed worshipped, in Ireland. One of our oldest traditions is that of the Well of Knowledge, but you are not likely to find that source since it is said now to lie either under the ocean or far below a deep lake. (We saw, earlier in this chapter, how Sionann, granddaughter of the sea god Manannán Mac Lir, found it, with disastrous results.)

Around that wonderful well grow the Hazel Trees of Knowledge, which drop their nuts into the water. The Salmon of Knowledge consumed those nuts, and thus became the holder of all wisdom, which would be transferred to whoever managed to catch and eat him. (The ancient ones knew well the value of fish for the brain.)

Wherever you go, you will find sacred springs (also known as tobair leighis or healing wells), each guarded and protected by its own nature spirit, but now almost all firmly dedicated to Christian saints. Such has been the influence of the Church indeed that somehow the inherent quality of the healing water has become inextricably associated with the power of this much later religion from another land. The water is thought to bestow its cures only as the gift of that religion, which is, emphatically, not the case. These healing wells, it should be realised, have nothing to do with Christianity and its rituals. They have everything to do with our generous natural world, which can provide help in so many ways for life's difficulties if we only embrace it.

Each healing well was known for its capacity to treat different illnesses or problems. Eyes, skin, hearing, infertility, even insanity have their own special sources that are believed to provide cures. They are to be found plentifully in the countryside and there are also many still in existence in our major cities, though by now they are usually well hidden from view. Dublin, for example, might still retain more than a hundred, while Cork and Limerick together have probably the same number. Often a street or road name gives the hint (Sunday's Well, Well Road, Patrickswell, Ladyswell, etc). And in the original Irish, tobar, meaning a well, is found in Ballintober, Tobermore, Tubberclare, Tubbercurry, etc. Any placenames like these should get your exploratory instincts up and buzzing.

Near Boyle in Co. Roscommon lies a well now dedicated to St Attracta, but formerly under the care of a powerful goddess, probably Brigit. A line of rounded stones resembling eggs are laid along the top of the surround. After drinking from the well, women hoping to have children should turn these reverently in a sunwise direction. You may remember from the previous chapter that the massive stones called beds of Diarmuid and Gráinne were used for the same hopeful purpose. Other wells have similar lines of rounded stones, which are used by sufferers to pass over their bodies for the healing of various afflictions. There is a belief that to deliberately turn these stones widdershins (that is, counter-sunwise) is to invoke dark spirits, to bring ill luck on someone you dislike. That is, of course, never, ever advisable. Putting an evil charm on someone almost always results in it returning sevenfold on the originator.

In the woods by Lough Hyne in Co. Cork are two healing wells, quite close to each other: Tobairín na Súl (Little Well of the Eyes) and Tobar na Sceabhrach (Well of the Slope). Each is credited with curing eye ailments, and clearly both draw their helpful waters from the same source. The trees and bushes surrounding these (hawthorn of course, but also rowan and holly) are hung with a fascinating array of pledges and petitions, in the form of ribbons, medals, tiny models, carved wooden crosses, woven rush crosses, even bus and ferry tickets. Each records a fervent wish or pledge.

Wells whose waters are considered good for treating the eyes are very common across Ireland, and will be found in every county. This is not surprising, dating from times that preceded opticians and eye tests, but contained plenty of opportunity for irritation, such as smoky turf fires. In Sligo, a hotel clerk avers that he always takes his children to the local eye well when they have sores or other problems: 'It's the best thing for them. Never fails.' The same qualities can be found at Tobar na Súl on the slopes of Slieve Sneacht on the Inishowen Peninsula in Co. Donegal. Not far away from that one is St Ultan's well, where children who do not start to walk at the usual age are taken for treatment. St Fintain's well in Sutton, Co. Dublin, cures not only eye ailments but stomach disorders too.

Almost as common as eye wells are those that cure warts, although these can also be treated in bullauns or hollowed-out stones. Once used for grinding corn, bullauns are now often found standing in quiet places, filled with rainwater. One such can be found carved out of the living rock high on a hill above Lissagriffin (note the lios in that name), just outside a famine graveyard.

Can you imagine the agony of severe toothache in the days before professional treatment at the hands of a dentist was available? Small wonder that there are several wells where some form of relief might be found. The Tooth Well at Glenisheen, just a little way north of the legendary Poulnabrone Dolmen in Co. Clare, is one such. It is a wonder in itself to find a well in the midst of that vast stone region, but this one, with its apparent ability to help with that dreadful endless nagging pain, has been known and resorted to for generations. It is difficult to see from a distance, as it is built of the same limestone paving as its surrounds and thus blends perfectly

into the landscape. The tiny well has a curved, sheltering roof and a ledge on which are placed small offerings like coins – and an occasional toothbrush! Ladywell at Balbriggan in north Co. Dublin was another source resorted to for relief from a nagging tooth.

There is a very strong belief, even in today's world of advanced medical treatments, that the water from a particular well of healing can achieve wonders. Is there any basis for these beliefs? Well yes, there probably is. Undoubtedly, many of these sources contain higher than usual quantities of partic-ular minerals that could assist with certain health conditions. Sulphur, for example, still used today for skin complaints; iron for ailing children; and so on.

One of the most interesting healing wells is Tobar na Galt or Well of the Insane, in Kerry. This has been known since ancient times as the place to go if your brain was afflicted – possibly by a charm being thrown on you by a druid, which could easily happen if you vexed him. He could cast a twist of straw in your face, mutter a few strange words, and there you would be, completely out of your mind. However, if you went to this secluded valley (known as Gleann na Galt, from the fame of its waters), drank from the spring and ate of the watercresses that grew there, you would be cured. That belief dates back thousands of years. It was duly recorded by the Christian monks when they arrived in the fifth century, although probably with raised eyebrows and a polite cough of skepticism.

Now, to bring in the science: When the water from this spring was tested some years ago, it was found to contain a high level of lithium, a mood-stabilising medicine used to treat certain mental illnesses. Clearly the wise ones of old knew about that, long before laboratories, experiments and scientific analysis came up with the same solution. Isn't that worth keeping in mind? Why do we always assume that we are the only generation ever to know anything, and that our forefathers were to be pitied for their ignorance? The truth is that they knew and understood far more of the natural world and its benefits than we are ever likely to learn.

Rituals connected with healing magic – making several circles around the well, saying prayers, leaving a rounded stone as offering – are practised at many sites, and are Christianised versions of the very ancient rituals that our ancestors would have used to petition or thank the gods. Circling sunwise, chanting praise, giving gifts – these are still practised in many countries (the faithful, for example, climb to the Yellow God above Kathmandu in Nepal each morning, singing and bringing food for the Buddhist monks). Christian rites are in reality just another variation of the old beliefs.

It should be noted that the water from any sacred well should only be used for healing purposes. It should never be used for casual matters, like slaking thirst or washing off the mud gathered on your trek to the spring. Tradition holds that if they are shown disrespect, the guardian spirits will take action, and the wells may disappear. It is claimed that there were once three such sources near Donoughmore in Co. Cork, all dedicated to St Lachteen, but two of them upped and moved when a young woman washed her feet there, insulting Themselves beyond bearing. They eventually reappeared at Grenagh, some miles away, but it is not known whether they carried their healing powers with them.

St David's Well in Co. Waterford is said to have been very beneficial for headaches or migraines, but here again folklore records that disrespect shown caused this to move.

There is a holy well called Tobar Cinín Dáibhidh in the townland of Woodhouse, situated in the corner of a field. People say that the well was originally further up the field. One day, a Major Fitzgerald washed his face in the well, and from that second, it started to dry, until it was as dry as the field. Then it sprang up in the field further down, and it is there to this day.

That story emphasises the reverence with which these sacred wells were regarded. Magical in their springing forth and constant supply, it was not to be wondered at if they or their guardian spirits chose to move to another location on a whim or at a perceived offence. Care needs to be taken, therefore, that this vital source of help in sickness should never be insulted.

To see a fish or an eel – or even a frog – in the well that you visit, by the way, may give you a shock at first, but is considered very fortunate indeed, and a sure sign that a cure will occur or that your wish will be granted.

It is said that if a person has some disease, goes to a holy well, and sees a fish in it, he is sure to be cured.

SEE THAT ISLAND ON THE HORIZON?

Small islands lying offshore are often seen as abodes of the Good People, since they are of our world yet not of it: you have to leave this land and cross the water to reach them. One of the most famous is Skellig Michael, close to the Kerry coast and recognised for thousands of years as a sacred place. It has been made even more famous in recent times by its participation (much against its will, one imagines) in *Star Wars* movies. Generally regarded as an old abode of monks, in reality its history goes back far further, into the mists of time. When the Celts first invaded Ireland, one of their noble number who died on the way was buried on Skellig Michael, indicating that it was a sacred and honoured place even then, long before Christianity had risen in the east. Besides the well-known beehive huts of the monks, there are older archaeological findings that show a far earlier occupation, including a very old staircase indeed on the less sheltered, more difficult of access side of the island.

Skellig Michael is in fact the last point on an ancient energy or ley line of power, stretching from the Middle East right up to this rocky kingdom on the edge of the explored world as it was then. Known as the Apollo–Michael Axis, it begins in the ancient city of Jerash, an important Byzantine/ Graeco-Roman centre, and moves up through Delos, Athens, Delphi, San Michele, Mont St Michel and St Michael's Mount, before finishing at Skellig. The southeastern points along this energy line are mostly dedicated to the sun god Apollo, while those towards the northwest tend to have Archangel Michael as their acknowledged saint. Over thousands of years, sanctuaries and places of worship sprang up along the axis, born of the recognition by their builders of the power contained therein. The ley or energy line, however, precedes many religions and many beliefs. There is so much we do not yet know about these fascinating lines of power, but it seems very likely that those who built our Irish megaliths had a good knowledge of where and how to find them and positioned their ritual sites accordingly.

Skellig, like Newgrange, is now on everyone's bucket list to visit, and for that reason you are unlikely to have it to yourself, as you should do to experience its power. The surrounding seas play their part too, sheltering it from invasion in bad weather. Perhaps the best way to appreciate it in comparative peace is to take one of the trips around the island when the seas are calm, which would allow you to marvel at its dizzying heights and frighteningly steep steps without actually having to climb them. (It is definitely not a place for those with vertigo.) By sailing around it, you can also enjoy the sight of the delightful puffins that nest there in the summer, taking flight from the crags to find food at sea and bring it back to their young in the burrows. And, of course, you would be making the circle of power, which is always a good idea.

And then there is legendary Hy Brasil, the Isle of the Blest, surely a home of the Good People. This has been such a strong tenet of belief down through the ages that it was marked on maps from as early as 1325 right down to the nineteenth century as lying off our west coast. St Brendan is of course supposed to have visited it, as did various sea captains. TJ Westropp, a Clare historian, claimed to have seen it several times, the last as late as 1872. It is said to appear now and again, whenever it pleases, arising out of a mist and showing amazing details of its wooded hills and tall towers, before it sinks out of sight again. It is always worth looking out to sea, especially at sunset, in case you might be lucky enough to catch a glimpse.

Hy Brasil is often equated with that magical world of the Good People, Tír na nÓg, the Land of Youth. Here the sun always shines, there is no growing old and everyone is supremely happy. Small wonder then that many dream of sailing out to find it, to see at last those wonderful ráths with their doors flung wide and golden torchlight gleaming out while the music sounds in welcome. However, the Good People guard its shores well – even if you did succeed in landing, it is unlikely you would ever return.

All small offshore islands are magical though, especially when seen at sunset. To travel to one, sit on its shore and look across at the mainland is to feel detached from all the worries of everyday modern life, to become part of an earlier time. Listen to the voices that echo around you and slip away into Their world for a little while. Don't you owe it to yourself?

CHAPTER VIII

WATCH FOR THE CHANGING SEASONS

Although Themselves are usually elusive, and rarely heard or glimpsed, there are certain times of year when the veil between our world and the Otherworld is at its thinnest, and They may walk abroad amongst us. Samhain, Midwinter, Imbolc, Bealtaine, Midsummer and Lughnasa are all ancient festivals marking the movement of the sun and the seasons. At these times above all, the Gentry are inclined to come a little closer to us humans, principally to check on what we are doing, and whether it is for the good of the land that is their principal care.

These days, the majority of us tend not to pay much if indeed any attention to the changing seasons. Farmers of course have always kept a close eye, as they have to. For them it is vital to know when the last date for planting is approaching, the possibility of a good dry week for harvesting, the likelihood of the first frost setting in, the length of the day itself, the need to bring cattle or sheep into safety. For the rest of us, though, it doesn't matter anything like it used to in older times. We might watch the forecast on television at night, given out in a friendly manner from an urban studio by a smiling girl in a summery dress whatever the season, with perhaps a nice map to show clouds and the sun. We don't even look out the window most of the time to check. Instead we rely on our modern trappings that protect us from any need so to do. Good clothing and footwear, a secure roof over our heads, food always available in supermarkets, cars to take us out in all weathers – what need have we of knowing what season it is, and what the year is doing?

Except for high days and holidays of course. Hallow-E'en, Christmas, Mayday, Midsummer, Lughnasa and others are still special occasions in our lives. We notice them because we take a break from the everyday and often indulge in pleasant activities, but without any real idea of why we are doing it. There is no chance that we'll forget Christmas or Hallow-E'en, as commercial interests, with their determined marketing departments and advertising campaigns, will ensure that we are reminded in good time.

But those activities are the very last remains of what were formerly intrinsic parts of our yearly round, markers to be observed as the sun gained or lost, as the nights became shorter or longer, as the weather changed, affecting everything that was important to our lives. We have always been a rural country, depending on our flocks and crops to supply our needs.

Even a few generations ago, your great-grandparents would have sensed when a storm was brewing, known when rain was on the way, been ready for the right day to plant the potatoes.

We should still have those instincts, that recognition of what the weather and the seasonal changes are brewing, but we have lost so much. Our children now look to their mobile phones to find out what is going on, instead of talking to people and taking notice of what is going on around them. We are increasingly living in a virtual world, outside of the real one. Social media tell us what to think, and we have all but forgotten the actual, natural world out there.

The Otherworld, however, has not and does not. Remember that our spirit ancestors, those who dwell in the fairy forts and the caves, in the hills and the forests, have always had one primary task above all – to care for this land they love. For them, each season in its turn is honoured and celebrated – the spring with its joyously fresh, green leaves; the summer with its generous crops and flowers; the autumn with its changing colours and the richness of fruits and nuts to be gathered; and the winter with its promise of dark softness and rest, a sleep while growth bides its time underground, waiting for the next spring. It is at the seasons' changes, marked by their festivals, that the veil is thinnest between Their world and ours. They come out at these times to walk among us and see how we are caring for our natural heritage.

At a time when that natural world is under more threat than ever before (principally due to our greed for convenient living and our total disregard for its consequences), it really does behove us to remember out roots, recall our origins, look to the land and the sky and see what they are telling us. We shouldn't have to switch on the nine o'clock news to see what the weather is doing. We should go outside, see if the stars are out or if it's cloudy, check from which direction the wind is blowing, look up at the moon to see which phase it has reached. When was the last time you looked for different constellations in the night skies or curtseyed in respect to the new moon?

The ancient traditional festivals of Ireland were held for a purpose, and our ancestors marked them with special celebrations to ensure Themselves would be good to us in the seasons ahead. Go mbéirimid beo ar an am seo arís – 'that we may be alive at this time again'. That's not just a glib saying – it meant a lot in the past, and it certainly should now.

The old Irish year was originally divided in half: winter starting at Samhain, the first day of November, and summer beginning with Bealtaine or May Day. Later came Imbolc at the start of February, marking the start of spring (earlier here than in many other countries), and Lughnasa at the beginning of August signifying the start of the harvest season, either giving food for the long winter months or in bad years failing, threatening starvation. Midsummer and Midwinter were seen as important points too, marking the turning of the sun in the skies, gradually increasing its strength and length of hours with which it blessed us, or decreasing slowly until the dark nights became longer than the short winter day.

SAMHAIN

It might seem strange to have the New Year beginning when the trees change colour and the leaves begin to fall, but it made sense in ancient Ireland. The wise ones knew that, like a child growing in the womb, seeds must lie in the ground for

Ripe apples, ready for gathering.

a time before coming up into the open world, and we all need a time of thought and preparation before starting the work of the year. Since winter is a quiet time anyway for crops and animals, and the weather encourages more staying indoors in shelter, this is an ideal time for looking inward, almost hibernating, and recouping our strength before setting out to meet the challenges of spring and summer. It's only since modern technology has allowed us to ignore the dark and the cold that we began to lose the old tried-and-trusted ways of matching our activities to the seasons.

The spirits of the Otherworld are very close at Samhain, and it was the custom for many centuries to lay out small dishes of food for them and for any of our own people who may have passed on. That way, they would know we honoured and thought of them at this important time. It's a nice thing to do still.

Since it's the start of the New Year, this is also a time for wondering what the twelve months ahead will bring, and it is from this that most of the traditional customs of Samhain stem. (Hallow-E'en is the Christianised term, meaning the eve of All Hallows or All Saints.) What do you remember of celebrations at this time in your childhood? A bonfire? Bobbing for apples, or trying to catch one with your teeth as it swings from the rafters? Placing hazelnuts close to the fire, to see which will break and leap out first? Dressing up in ghostly garments and going 'trick or treating' around the neighbourhood? You might see these as childish games, but there is a rock-solid core of practical belief and tradition behind every one of those.

The ritual bonfire is part of ancient Irish practice, kindled and lit by druids on the great festivals to mark the importance of the time and date. These ritual bonfires were composed of nine sacred woods, carefully gathered and assembled until the chief druid struck spark from flint and kindled the flames. All household fires had to be completely extinguished before this happened, and only afterwards re-lit from the bonfire. That's no small matter when you consider that the fire was the source of heat, cooking, safety and everything else, and normally was not allowed to go out from one end of the year to the other.

The nine sacred woods? We discussed this in detail in an earlier book (*Old Ways, Old Secrets*, O'Brien Press, 2015), but here again is the list quoted in MacNeill's *The Silver Bough*:

Choose the willow of the streams,
Choose the hazel of the rocks,
Choose the alder of the marshes,
Choose the birch of the waterfalls,

Choose the rowan of the shade,
Choose the yew of resilience,
Choose the elm of the brae,
Choose the oak of the sun.

Only eight given, as you have doubtless noted. That's the strength of a spell – the final piece is only put in by the practitioner at the very last minute. It doesn't do to spread the knowledge outside the inner circle. MacNeill suggests that the missing link could have been holly, ash or pine. Others consider hawthorn, with its strong Otherworld links, to be the most likely contender.

When Henry VIII endeavoured to expunge the Church of Rome from England, he naturally tried to get rid of many of their practices as well. Among these was Hallow-E'en, the former Samhain. Since the people still clung to the tradition of the bonfire, however, his advisers suggested commemorating Guy Fawkes instead, an unsuccessful incendiarist who attempted to blow up the Houses of Parliament. And so now England's children make a bonfire on 5 November and burn a stuffed image known as a Guy. It does appear strange to have such a relatively minor villain and failed attempt commemorated with such energy, but when you realise that it is really Samhain or Hallow-E'en that is being celebrated, it becomes more understandable.

Since the Good People are believed to be out and about at this time, it was always considered a good opportunity to beg for a vision of the future, to try to discover what lay in store in the year ahead. Apples, now ripened and carefully gathered,

were used for several foretelling practices. Catching a swing-
ing apple in your teeth could mean triumph in your endeav-
ours if you try hard enough, similarly trying to secure one
floating in a tub of water. The skilful might try to peel an apple
in one single piece, and throw the resultant coil of skin over
their left shoulder, to see if it made the initial of someone who
might become important in their lives. Placing nuts by the fire
and naming each one for those trying to see the future, could
be interpreted in different ways, depending on which cracked
or leaped first and which way it went.

A rough loaf shaped of flour might be placed on the table
with a piece of fruit hidden inside. Turns would be taken
at cutting a slice very carefully. The one who uncovered the
hidden fruit would then have to see if it could be removed
by the teeth without collapsing the entire shape into ruin. It
boded well for future success if you could achieve this.

Most famous was perhaps the bairín breac or speckled loaf,
which contained several objects to denote your future pros-
pects. The official clues were a ring, a rag, a pea, a bean and
a stick, indicating respectively marriage, single status, riches,
poverty and a beating. The excitement when each person cut
a slice to see what fortune they would get would have been
considerable. This tradition is still very much in existence
today, with every store and supermarket piling shelves high
with the Hallow-E'en barmbrack (although modern health
and safety regulations have cut down somewhat on the
hidden contents). A similar practice existed in France with
the gateau des rois of 6 January, which had small china kings
hidden in the cake.

Ready for Samhain – barmbrack, hazelnuts and apples by the fire.

Enormous fun, these fortune-telling games, but serious too, when there was no better way of discovering what might lie ahead.

Next, how about the now extremely commercialised practice of kids dressing up as ghosts and evil spirits and going around the neighbourhood threatening tricks if a treat is not forthcoming? Well, there was a very good reason for that too, with the night that was in it, the time when Themselves might well be walking abroad and checking on us to see if we are behaving properly.

It works like this: Since all kinds of spirits are around on the ancient New Year's Eve (31 October), and among them mischievous ones who love to play tricks, you might well find them heading up your laneway, bent on causing trouble. They might open gates, let out the cattle or sheep, throw mud at the windows, terrify the poultry. But if they chance to see a ghostly figure ahead of them, uttering frightening cries and hammering

235

at a front door, they think, 'Oh, one of the others got here ahead of me,' and so off they go to find someone else to scare. So there is a very old justification for trick-or-treating, despite its undeniable over-commercialisation these days (every supermarket packed with displays of sweets and treats for householders to buy in advance, special costumes on sale, for example).

It was, in olden times, a very important protection against malevolence and misfortune. Because those who might mean you ill can be abroad at Samhain just as much as the more benevolent spirits and it's wise to watch your step. In earlier times, nobody would think of going out alone once darkness fell. Once the cock crew for New Year's Day, 1 November, you were safe. Something to remember if you are reading this as Samhain approaches: If you are, unfortunately, trapped by some mischief-minded spirits, remember again the same trick as at the fairy fort – hastily turn your coat inside out, and you may escape.

There is one last way of trying to discover what the future holds, although it is not necessarily recommended for the fearful. It applies mostly to young women who, predictably, would like to know who their future partner might be. Late at night, sit alone in a darkened room in front of a mirror, with just a lighted candle either side of the glass. Stare into the mirror while brushing your hair, and wait. You may see a face look over your shoulder. You may see nothing at all. Or – you may see something entirely unexpected. Remember that Themselves are abroad on this night of all nights, and not averse to playing a little trick or two on those seeking to know more than they should.

MIDWINTER

Since the establishment of Christianity on this island around the fifth century, we have tended to celebrate 25 December as the major winter feast, marking the birth of Christ, but formerly it would have been Midwinter around 21 December, the all-important time of the solstice, when the sun finally turns from the dark to grow stronger again with the promise of still far-off summer. Despite current belief, it might not necessarily be precisely the calendar date of 21 December, but simply around that time of year.

The druids, the wise ones of a far older Ireland, had studied the stars and the skies for a lifetime and could predict pretty accurately when the actual time was that the sun relented and turned back, and all could celebrate. Many of the greatest stone monuments that survive from ancient times were oriented to face the southeast, where the solstice sun rose in late December. It has always been a supremely important time. Today we still realise with pleasure that the year has turned at last. 'Ah, the days are drawing out now,' is a frequently heard phrase (despite the bitter knowledge that Ireland in January and February can throw some of its most miserable weather at us, and usually does!).

Now that the people knew with joy the turning point had been reached, they could take the risk of breaking out some of their carefully hoarded stores of food, making a feast with apples, nuts, blackberries, honey, perhaps using some of the painstakingly ground flour to make bread. In today's world, when we are so sure of finding anything we need in the supermarket, it is as well sometimes to recall days when only good management, a bit of luck and the careful stocking of shelves and stores in the autumn could ensure survival.

Despite the plenty on offer in the shops nowadays, it is still a good idea to gather blackberries and apples as they ripen, and make a pot or two of jam or jelly to put on your own shelves, thereby continuing the link with those who did the same before you. It's good for the soul as well as the body. You can be sure that Themselves are watching, and nodding in approval.

Another custom at Midwinter, when the more mischievous of the Otherworld spirits might be expected to visit, was to change clothes, to dress up as each other in order to confuse things. In courtly gatherings, in particular, the lords and ladies took delight in changing both garments and placings with their servants, so that the scullion took the top of the table as the Lord of Misrule for the night, and his master went to the bottom. To make it more convincing, the Lord of Misrule would be given an imitation crown to wear during the feasting, and others would follow suit with quickly fashioned wreaths and caps to suit their new social position for that evening. Anything there sound familiar? Yes, it is still practised at today's Christmas dinners, where everybody wears paper crowns and other hats, collected from the crackers, although few know the origin of the custom.

Two other customs observed at this time of year are also linked to the turning of the year. One, hunting the wren, is now commonly practised on 26 December (St Stephen's Day in Ireland) and the other, Women's Christmas, on 6 January.

Hunting the wren is a curious survivor from a much older time, and still holds vestiges of the ancient practice. Groups of children, disguised in rags, carry the model of a wren on a branch from house to house, singing songs and collecting money or sweets.

The wren, the wren, the king of all birds
St Stephen's Day he was caught in the furze.
Knock at the knocker, ring at the bell,
Please give us a copper for singing so well!

In some locations, notably Dingle in Kerry, it has become a major festival. Here, all ages take part, dressed in a wide variety of costumes, including ones of made of plaited straw and even a white horse costume. They travel through the town, making music as they go and raising money for charity.

What is behind it? Nobody knows for sure, but we would suggest that it may be linked to the ancient tradition of the corn king. In many cultures, it was believed that the god of

Wren boys in Dingle.

fertility and growth must die and go underground at this time, before he can rise again to see that the crops sprout and come into full fruition once more. The idea was seized on by the Christian Church later and used for its tale of the death and rebirth of Christ. In the classic legend of Proserpina, it is a maiden who descends into the underworld and is only allowed to return for half the year, but in other cultures it is the current king. Here in Ireland, it is likely that 'the Wren Boys' carry the model of the king of birds to indicate that he has died, and therefore will be able to rise again in the spring.

Women's Christmas is another strange survivor, celebrated on 6 January or Twelfth Night. It is popularly regarded as an opportunity for hard-working housewives to take a break at last, after the rigours of the Christmas festivities, but it goes back further than that. In some parts of Ireland, particularly around Connemara and Donegal, which have held on to the old ways for longer, it is still taken seriously. One elderly woman recalled that when she was young, the men were banished to walk the fields for the day, while the women gathered in rare peace and quiet to drink tea, eat good food, tell stories and generally enjoy themselves.

These days, with modern commercialism, it's a big night out for girls of all ages, with special shows being put on at local theatres and clubs, and festivities being continued long into the night. Some women even host Women's Christmas breakfast parties. The only part men are allowed to take is that of performers at the special shows, and sometimes this can pose more of a risk than an artist might expect. Women have the liberty on this special day to be who they want, to do what they want, without any fear of male disapproval (we don't need to go into the details of the Greek maenads and what they did to the young men they crowned briefly as kings and then disposed of, but the link is there).

Again, we don't know for sure, but it is likely that this is a survivor from the very earliest times, when all followers of the female goddesses came together to celebrate their identity and revel in their uniqueness. And it's still here, still celebrated, honouring our female spirit ancestors.

IMBOLC

The first day of February is celebrated in Ireland as Imbolc, the real start of spring, with lambs on the way and the ewes coming into milk. Around this time too, the earliest flowers appear – the bright yellow celandine, the paler primrose, sometimes even the first hazel catkins. This was a vitally important time for those who had spent the last few weeks of winter in scarcity and privation, since most of their stores would have been used up, and milk products in particular would not have lasted out. New milk was a boon for both young lambs and their human owners, and a cause for celebration.

This day has only recently been incorporated into the Irish calendar as a bank holiday, but has since time immemorial been firmly dedicated to Brigit, the young goddess who cares for all animals and new growth. To honour her, the people would decorate sacred wells and hold gatherings of praise, while troupes of entertainers, known as Biddy Dancers, would go from settlement to settlement extolling her virtues. A model of the goddess, called the brídeóg, was carried on these journeys.

Biddy Dancers celebrating Imbolc at Muckross.

The practice has almost died out now, but you can still find Biddy Dancers in Kerry at the beginning of the month, moving about from pub to pub and occasionally from house to house, as they would have done a century ago, receiving a warm welcome, food and drink at each halt. Stately Muckross House in Killarney is often one of their starting points.

Another ancient custom attached to Imbolc, and still practised today (with heavy Christian overlay of course), is the creation of Brigit's Crosses in rushes or straw. This little woven talisman served as a good luck symbol and was hung in various places around the home and animal sheds to discourage unfriendly spirits and bad luck. In shape it represents the swastika, a very ancient symbol indeed, representing the power of the sun. The design can vary from place to place, depending on the weaving of the rushes, but the overall result is much the same. You can still find ancient, dusty examples hanging from the rafters of old farmhouses or over the doors of stables.

It is good to see them still made today, in school classrooms and even in craft groups, although of course now the Christian Church has firmly laid its hand on them, declaring them to originate with Saint Brigid, their much later alteration (denigration?) of the timeless and all-powerful goddess. However, the Irish government has only recently decreed that the weaving of this cross is to receive formal state recognition as part of our living cultural heritage. So it's still here, still surviving from ancient times, regardless of how recent vested interests have worked their interpretation of its origins.

Another venerable tradition connected with Imbolc is the putting out of the brat Bríde or Brigit's Cloak, on the eve of 1 February. Today, it is more likely to be a scarf or a length of cloth than a cloak, but in any case, it is spread on a bush as near as possible to the home and left out overnight. It is thought that as the goddess passes by on the eve of her festival, she will bestow power on it. Next morning it is brought in, carefully folded up and kept for use against illnesses such as sore throats or fevers. Placed around the sufferer's neck, it is believed to aid a rapid cure. Although this custom rather fell out of use in the past half-century, it is now enjoying a revival through popular discussions on social media – a sign that perhaps such new technological advances can in fact be used to encourage a return to the old ways.

BEALTAINE

The first day of May is the most important in the ancient Irish calendar, marking the coming of summer with all its promise of sunlight and growth. This and Samhain were the two original

The ancient roads sometimes
become visible to our eyes at
Bealtaine.

divisions of the year, and while the end of October marks the onset of the dark months, when all goes underground, Bealtaine (Bel-tine or Bright Fire) celebrates the return of warmth and light. The festival honours the sun, with processions to the highest hills and ritual bonfires. In a primarily agricultural society, this has traditionally been the busiest time of year for farmers, with everything depending on a strong and helpful sun. The moon has always been honoured in Ireland, and its phases carefully noted for various tasks, such as sowing or reaping, but undoubtedly the sun was worshipped as the giver (or withholder) of successful crops, healthy families, good flocks and herds and a guarantee of full barns for the winter to come.

As one of the two greatest festivals of the ancient Irish year, Bealtaine is a time when the veil is thinnest between our world and the Otherworld, and the Good People often choose this time to travel the countryside, using the old roads. These ancient trackways have long since disappeared from human view, but they reappear on May Eve, stretching out like silver pathways across boglands and hillsides, or even across lakes, where the road is made of silver moonlight. If you should chance to come across one of these secret roads, it's best not to step onto it. If you do, there is every chance you will not be able to leave it again.

A fascinating practice is still observed at Cathair Crobh Dearg, an ancient ritual site situated between the Paps of Danu, two softly rounded mountains standing high above the Cork–Kerry border. Once a powerful caiseal or royal fort, it has become known over the centuries for the power of the water from its spring or natural well. This water is different though – it is not for human good, but for animal welfare. People travel long distances to it, arriving from dawn onwards on the first day of May, sometimes bringing smaller animals with them to drink from the source, more often carrying bottles or flagons so that they can bring the water home to aid their flocks and herds.

The belief is as strong today as it ever was. ''Tis not for ourselves, you understand,' says an elderly man, creaking out of his battered car and pulling an old lemonade bottle from behind the seat. ''Tis for the animals, that's what it is. It's only for them.'

In earlier centuries, those climbing to this site on the all-important day would enjoy a celebration of the coming of summer, holding impromptu picnics, making music, generally 'bringing in the May'. Naturally enough, the Catholic Church disapproved of such enjoyments, fearing (probably with good reason) that things would get a little out of hand. They did their best to forbid these observances and beliefs, but finding they were making little progress, they did the next best thing and introduced statues and crosses and other Christian motifs, as well as ritual circlings of the caiseal with associated prayers.

Today, if you get there early enough, you will see the old ways in progress, with water being gathered for the animals; later in the day, the Church supporters arrive and Mass is celebrated. Both have their followers; both believe in their own way of doing things. The Cathair tolerates the newer religious symbols, but continues to gaze out across the wide landscape as it has done for centuries, keeping its millennia of memories to itself.

There are many everyday customs associated with May Day too, most of them linked to avoiding bad luck or ill-wishers. It was always thought risky to let anyone visit your home on that morning, in case they took away the milk from your cows, or even your ability to make butter. There are many stories of old women being seen sweeping a neighbour's grassy fields with a birch or heather broom, with the purpose of removing all the good luck with the morning dew. Sometimes it might be a hare that was seen, running to and fro in those fields. In that case, the only option was to load a gun with a silver sixpence and try to hit it, as it was undoubtedly a wise woman in disguise, with the theft of your butter and milk in mind, and only a silver sixpence could injure it. Such stories often end with a visit to a neighbouring cottage where an old woman is found with an injury explainable only by that silver coin.

It's understandable that there would be fears and preventative actions where dairy products were concerned, since meat was a rare luxury in most communities, and household diets depended heavily on milk, butter and cheese. The coming of summer meant a plentiful supply of these, so it was important to keep an eye on anyone seeking to steal your supply, whether by outright theft or by magical means.

May is when the fairy tree, the hawthorn, comes into splendid bloom, turning fairy forts and whole hillsides into a frothing mist of white. Branches of hawthorn were cut (May Day is the only occasion when it is permitted to cut this tree for the right purposes) and placed over the lintels of houses and sheds, to protect the residents from evil influences. Similarly, flowers were gathered into little nosegays and bouquets and fastened

Placing nosegays of flowers on doors is an old May Day custom.

to front doors or placed on doorsteps, and small bunches were even fastened to the harnesses of horses. This was still being done as late as the 1960s in Ireland, but is seen less and less as the years go on, and more countryside disappears beneath tarmac and concrete. It's a good and powerful thing to do, though, and should always be practised on May Day, even if you only twine a length of grass into a circle and hang it on a doorknob. In that way, you too celebrate the coming of the welcome days of summer.

Is there any female out there who doesn't know how important it is to bathe your face in dew on May morning? Countless generations of women have done so, trusting in the old belief that to do this is to ensure lifelong beauty and health. There is no reason why the male population shouldn't do it too – after all, healthy skin and natural good looks are desirable for everyone surely?

MIDSUMMER

This is the time when the sun is at its height, the days are at their longest and the nights very short indeed. Those who tend the land are looking anxiously at their crops, wondering if the weather will allow them to bring it to full and successful harvest a month or so later.

In older times, without all the benefits of modern technology, life was naturally governed by the movements of the sun, and this turning point in the year was supremely important. The actual date, like that of Midwinter, is somewhere around 21 June, but can vary a couple of days either way. Again, the druids, the wise ones of old, would have scanned the skies and known the precise date for rituals associated with the summer solstice. Principal among those rituals was the sacred fire, lit on the highest hilltop available, so that it was nearest to the sun. Honouring the sun god and at the same time banishing any evil spirits that might ill-wish the all-important harvest was its purpose. Naturally enough, this was also an occasion for gathering together, feasting, making music and dancing. Later in the year, there would be little time for that, once the work of bringing in the crops began.

Christianity of course, trying yet again to move significant dates away from association with pagan rituals, tried to make St John's Eve, 23 June, the appropriate day to celebrate. And it is on the night of 23 June that one ancient practice still continues, most of all in the county and city of Cork. Here it is not called Midsummer, nor yet St John's Eve, but Bonfire Night.

If you just happen to be flying in to Cork airport that evening, you will see the strangest of eerie effects, something so out of the ordinary, you might rub your eyes and wonder if you are dreaming. Grey billows of smoke, uprising columns on every side, throughout the city and out in the countryside beyond. Wildfires? Surely not in a county renowned for its rainfall. Clouds? No, it can't be clouds. What is it?

Well, it's Bonfire Night, observed by children of today's world who know nothing about ancient traditions or pagan rituals, disregard history books and play in their own heedless way, regardless of old customs. But yet they know that on this one night they should – indeed, they are compelled to – go out, gather firewood, timber, even old pieces of furniture, and make the biggest bonfire they can. Asked why, they will

Bonfire Night at midsummer in Cork.

look nonplussed and say, 'It's what you do on the twenty-third. It's Bonna Night, isn't it?' Whole families come out and sit around the fire while the kids rush hither and thither, dragging new fuel to the flames. It's practised in the country as well as the city, but it is in the urban environment that you really see the observation of an ancient rite brought right into the modern day.

Dangerous? Of course. Distinctly risky? Certainly. Haven't the authorities done anything? Yes, they have. Dire warnings go out for weeks beforehand from the fire brigade. Sensible, safe, well-meant events are organised on a secure site, where risks are kept to a minimum and the attendees are fairly strictly regulated. So that's all right then, isn't it?

No, not exactly. You do get crowds coming to these organised events, but the old illegal ones still continue, in housing estates, on back streets, on top of any of the hills in which the city abounds. The old ways must be observed, even if its participants have no clear idea of what they are doing. There is certainly little notion that they are perpetuating one of our oldest rituals. But after all, they probably do have an interest in the sun continuing to shine down until the end of the summer holidays. The old customs survive in the most unexpected places.

LUGHNASA

When we arrive at the beginning of August, the final stage of the farmer's year is in sight, as the crops ripen. Lughnasa, named after the god Lugh, is not therefore a harvest festival in any sense of the word except that of anticipation. We might think of summer as a time of plenty, but in fact it was often a hungry time for our ancestors, as the winter stores would have long given out, and the new harvest was not yet ready for reaping.

This was (and still is) the festival when climbing to the top of a sacred hill or mountain was all-important, to beg the gods to be kind to the harvest. August can be a wicked month, with unreliable weather, when heavy downpours or even thunderstorms can occur, with the risk of wrecking carefully tended crops. Toiling up to the crown of the hill and making offerings to the gods was seen as the best way to ensure the goodwill of those Otherworld spirits who controlled the sun and the weather generally.

Climbing up Croagh Patrick on the Sunday nearest to 1 August is now a huge religious event, with thousands making their cautious way up the stony, winding path to the summit, some 764 metres (2,507 feet) up. Some even do it barefoot. The clergy make their way up too, and celebrate Mass at the summit. Definitely a Christian rite then?

Well, no. For thousands of years before the Roman religion emerged, let alone reached these shores, believers in the old ways and the kindliness or otherwise of the sun god have been climbing this ancient mountain at this time of year. It was originally known as Cruachán Aigle, which is taken to refer to one of our older and darker gods of the harvest, Crom Dubh or Crom Cruach, already mentioned in Chapter V. He, you will recall, was revered and feared before the lighter, younger, kinder sun god, Lugh of the Long Arm, entered the pantheon of Otherworld spirits. Climbing to the top of his mountain at this time to make offerings was seen as a sensible way of trying to protect the coming harvest.

The long trek up
to the summit of
Croagh Patrick.

There are traces of ancient structures and stones at the summit that predate Christianity, and many more are scattered all around the slopes below, showing that this has been a sacred site since prehistory. It was a zealous monk, writing a Life of Patrick long after that holy man had departed this Earth, who composed a stirring tale that featured Patrick climbing to the top of the mountain and casting out a serpent into a lake far below. (Serpents, which in nature have never been seen in Ireland, were, in Christian doctrine, a synonym for the old pagan ways. Wherever you find a saint casting one out, you can be sure that that's where old beliefs have been rigorously deleted or covered over.)

They climb to honour Crom in Kerry too, at Mount Brandon. To ensure good luck in the year ahead, hundreds gather in the little village of Cloghane on the day to make the arduous trek upwards. Brandon is actually named for Bran, a voyager of the ancient tales, but nowadays is generally attributed to Saint Brendan, who is said to have embarked on his legendary journey to the New World from a nearby creek (as did Tim Severin in the twentieth century, endeavouring to see if Brendan's voyage was really possible. He found that it was.).

A brief sidetrack might be permitted here on Brendan's voyage, since over and over, you hear of this enterprising monk 'discovering America'. How on earth could this be true? For a start, the most basic research indicates quite unambiguously that several explorers had not only found it but had established trade routes there, well before the dates suggested for Brendan. And, more conclusively, the actual records which give details of his journey state clearly that he only decides to go because he is told of another monk who has already made the trip there and back, and claimed to have converted many of the New Worlders while he was at it. Somehow those hard facts go unnoticed while everyone concentrates on the methods Brendan used to build his boat – the skins, the sewing, the amount of butter needed to oil the hides, etc. So we can remove Brendan's role as intrepid explorer of unknown lands, put him firmly into the category of eager follower in other people's wake, and carry on.

In the north of the country, 1 August is known as Blaeberry Sunday, possibly because of the pressure by colonising England to stamp out both the pagan and the Catholic rituals. This is the time of year when the wild fraocháns or bilberries ripen, and crowds go up into the hills to gather the tiny black fruit. It was customary for sweethearts to make little bracelets of these and give them to each other, but the rule was that the gifts had to be buried up there before you made your descent, as a thank you to Themselves. Buckets of fraocháns could be brought back though for those who could not make the ascent.

And a great fair of ancient origin is held at this time since far back before records began. Puck Fair in Killorglin has always been held on the same three days in August, known as the Gathering, the Fair Day and the Scattering. When the Catholic Church decided to take ten days out of the calendar back in 1582, the fair still held firmly to those days, even though they were now in the middle of the month rather than the beginning, at Lughnasa. The actual days appointed so long ago were the important ones, not a fiddling with the calendar thought up by someone in Rome.

Traditionally, the travelling people come to Killorglin from all sides in their caravans to trade horses and cattle, buy supplies and meet up with friends and relatives that they would not have seen since the previous year. They are joined by crowds of country folk and city dwellers too, all eager to enjoy the biggest event of the calendar year, when a wild mountain goat is crowned king with a golden crown, and hoisted up onto a platform high above the crowds in the town square. There he is feted and fed for the three days before being turned back to the hillsides once more. This custom continued up to very recently, with a young girl chosen as queen each year to place the crown on the goat's head (not easy with those viciously curving horns) before he spends his three days being spoiled rotten. However, modern feelings and social pressure have forced change, and now he is very briefly crowned and raised up so that all can see, before being swiftly brought down again. It might fit better with current views on the care of animals, but it is definitely not what it should be – the strong image of a pagan power figure presiding over his summer gathering throughout its traditional three days.

And so the circle of the seasons continues, hopefully with good crops to be gathered in before the autumnal collection of nuts, berries and apples is begun. Thankfully, the Good People have heard the prayers of their people and given them a good harvest. Now it must all be safely stored away in preparation for the end of the year and the coming of Samhain, when the Good People will once more emerge from their circles of power, the fairy forts.